Coronary?
Cancer?

God's Answer: Prevent It!

Dr. Richard O. Brennan

with

Helen Kooiman Hosier

Foreword by
Dr. Harold Manner

HARVEST HOUSE PUBLISHERS
Irvine, California 92714

Verses marked AMP are quoted from The Amplified Bible, Copyright © 1965 by Zondervan Publishing House.

Verses marked NASB are quoted from The New American Standard Bible, Copyright © The Lockman Foundation 1960, 1962, 1963, 1968, 1971, 1972, 1973, 1975, and are used by permission.

Verses marked NIV are quoted from The Holy Bible, New International Version, copyright © 1978 by The New York International Bible Society. Used by permission.

Verses marked TLB are quoted from The Living Bible, copyright © 1971 by Tyndale House Publishers, Wheaton, Illinois. Used by permission.

Acknowledgment is hereby given to information referred to in Nutrigenetics, Copyright 1975, Richard O. Brennan, published by M. Evans and Company, Inc. and by The New American Library, Inc.

CORONARY? CANCER? GOD'S ANSWER: PREVENT IT!

Copyright © 1979 by Richard O. Brennan

Published by Harvest House Publishers
Irvine, California 92714

Library of Congress Catalog Card Number #79-84719
ISBN 0-89081-181-4

Printed in the United States of America.

FOREWORD

"Very few people know what real health is because most are occupied with killing themselves slowly." So said Albert Szent-Gyorgyi, Nobel Prize Laureate.

The above words sound as if they could have been written by some health-food fadist who doesn't really understand the intricacies of the human body and the profound mechanisms involved in disease. But let me assure you that these words were written by a trained physician who has spent most of his professional life healing his patients.

From the time he was in professional school, Dr. Richard Brennan felt that there was something more to healing than what his professors taught him. However, it wasn't until tragedy struck his own family that these ideas really crystallized. The story of this personal drama is lucidly portrayed by Dr. Brennan in the early pages of this book.

He began to realize that true and thorough healing involved the physical, mental, and spiritual components of the human body. This is something that most practicing physicians all too frequently forget. Scattered throughout the pages of this book are quotations from the finest medical book ever written—the Holy Bible. These Scriptures should serve as an inspiration to every reader, whether healing physician or patient seeking healing. In a way this book reveals the inner man of Dr. Brennan. I have personally known him for years. He lives the way he writes. Patients who have him as their personal physician are among the most fortunate persons on earth.

Scientifically, the book is sound. The diets and treatment plans revolve around the hierarchy of body organization. The body is composed of organ systems which in turn are a collection of organs. These organs are a complex of individual tissue each of which is a collection of cells. The cell is not only the basic building block of the body but is also the entity which must be treated if the body is to heal itself of the dread diseases discussed in this book. This cellular therapy is new. It is part of what must be considered a new frontier in medicine.

It is a pleasure to know and to be able to count as my personal friend this outstanding physician. It is likewise a special pleasure to be able to provide this foreword to his book—a book that I predict will become a classic in the annals of medicine.

—Harold W. Manner, Ph.D.
Loyola University
Chicago, Illinois

CONTENTS

Foreword .... Dr. Harold Manner

Introduction .... Dr. R.O. Brennan

1. Cancer Is No Respecter of Persons 11

2. What Is Cancer? 23

3. Why Cancer? 47

4. Cancer Charade 71

5. Cancer's Companions 87

6. The What and Why of Coronary Disease 105

7. Magic Enzymes 127

8. Love Your Liver 143

9. Freedom from Fear 155

10. Cell-Assurance Program 173

11. Nutrition Plus 195

12. The Power of Prayer 211

Appendices 221

DEDICATION

Dedicated to the
indomitable spirit of Phyllis

INTRODUCTION

I wrote this book because I believe it is badly needed. Our country has desperate health problems. I wrote this book with the deepening conviction that our approach to the problem of cancer in this country is ineffectual, inadequate, and misdirected. It has failed. It is failing now.

It is not the desire of this author to detract in any way from the benefits of the great medical care that is given the actually ill patient. It is only hoped that there will be an increasing awareness in the medical profession and the government to rise to the needs of the chronically ill patient and assume the role of teacher and supporter of preventive measures that are so critically needed to enhance the great medical sick care that is being exhibited by the medical profession.

The public should be told; the public should know that the answer to cancer lies in preventing it. The individual must know that the primary answer to cancer is up to the individual himself. He must learn to use the magic of his own body's protective and healing mechanism—a divine gift from his Creator. He needs to know that the answer to cancer lies within the confines of his own metabolic processes.

It is evident that the battle against the increasing incidence of the chronic degenerative diseases has to be fought. It can only be won by massive preventive programs aimed at restoring every citizen's normal cell activities. America needs a *wellness-oriented* health-care approach.

Many of today's men of medicine are beginning to believe that our present sick-care system is headed for a catastrophic breakdown. They also believe that the next real medical breakthrough is the philosophy and practice of preventive medicine, for true health is impossible without restoration of meaningful health to the body, mind, and spirit.

We must not be fooled by the tendency of scientific researchers to look at one part of the body and think they will find the answer to cancer in one area. Cancer is not a local disease, and the malignancy epidemic cannot be solved by the microscopic study of the structures of abnormal tissues. Cancer is a disease that affects the entire body and must be considered as a total body problem.

We cannot restore the poor health of the body without the power of the God-given metabolic healing mechanism, which must function well at all times.

This book presents an innovative concept employing the cellular theory of disease based on the weakness of cells called "hypocellulosis" (a new term). Hypocellulosis is largely due to 1) poor genetic patterns, 2) malnutrition caused by "anutrientosis" (another coined term) and 3) "antinutrition" (another coined term). The inherent strength of the human cell is directly affected by these factors, and the proper care of the cell is the basis for improving health and immune processes of the body.

Anutrientosis, the condition of a generalized overall inclusive malnutrition state, is nearly universal among Americans due to the devitalizing and overprocessing of our food and the elimination of vital nutrients. The condition is further aggravated by antinutrition—poisoned air, water, and food that we take into our bodies.

This book points out that the metabolic imbalances resulting from hypocellulosis, anutrientosis, and antinutrition cause the metabolic dysequilibrium syndrome that comprises the chronic degenerative diseases and forms the common basis for our problems of today.

This book further points out that there is no way to have a healthy mind in an unhealthy body. It brings in the proper relationship between the body and the mind and emphasizes the significance of spiritual well-being. We have overlooked the interaction of spirit, mind, and body, and we need to look back to ancient medicine and to the scriptural teachings that, if followed, would have avoided much of what is happening to civilization today. We can then prevent much of what might happen to us in the future.

The pollution of air, body, and water affects our impaired cellular function, as the liver cannot detoxify all the additives in our food and other unnatural chemicals in our environment. Pollution and malnutrition lead to the sick cells that make up our sick tissues, organs, and glands.

We have reached such a state of pseudoscientific sophistication that we will not accept the empirical approach that can save our lives and prevent the high cost of our sick-care system. We have been misled by the scientific approach to the isolation and study of individual nutrients; we have failed to understand that the entire gamut of adequate nutrients is needed if we are to survive and stay healthy.

Suitable attention has not been paid to the entire cycle of nutrients that enter the body's system. The proper digestion of food must begin in the mouth and then continue in the stomach and the small intestine. Then we must have the proper "liverising" of our health-sustaining nutrients. One of the great tragedies of American medicine is that few physicians pay any attention to what their patients eat and drink. Very little attention is paid to the health-giving qualities of an optimum gastrointestinal system. Many doctors should go back to "alimentary school." They have overlooked the effect on the entire body if there is a breakdown of the body's ability to assimilate and utilize the materials that are put into the mouth.

Not only must the body break down and assimilate the smallest and finest components of food, but the body must also be capable of utilizing it at the cellular level. The biological cleanup crew must empty the trillions of wastebaskets and garbage pails every day.

This book presents a medical and preventive breakthrough because it employs the ultimate total approach to the chronic degenerative diseases, cancer, cardiovascular disease, and diabetes.

We cannot afford to wait for some miracle "cancer cure." We have nothing to lose and everything to gain by initiating a plan that can postpone and prevent the advent of our chronic degenerative diseases and our major causes of death: heart attacks, diabetes, and cancer.

The prescribing of chemicals that we know as drugs must be minimized. Nutritional eating routines should be employed, along with proper exercising programs necessary to improve the *quantity* and *quality* of the blood flow to the cells. It should contain all nutrients needed by each of those cells.

If we are to survive, we must take a fresh new look at preventing cancer, because it is too late once any of the chronic degenerative diseases are well-established. Supportive measures must then be employed. When we plan our anticancer campaign and formulate the preventive approach, we must look to all contributors of the functional breakdown in our cells. We must avoid all carcinogens, such as tobacco smoke, chemicalized food, and polluted air and water.

It is late, but we must awaken to the fact that we simply have to employ a total biocellular preventive-medicine approach with the needed spiritual and psychological measures that are necessary for full, happy health. We should remember that the rudiments of well-balanced metabolic processes will prevent the cancer that will kill.

Peace of mind does not come in capsules. Peace of mind comes from the inner qualities that are based on the soundness of body and mind that is in tune with God. There is more power in prayer than in a medical prescription.

—Dr. Richard O. Brennan
Associate Medical Director and Cofounder
Health Haven Clinic, Whale Point Retreat
Eleuthera, Bahamas

1

O Father, Thou has made
us so we can damage or can
deliver ourselves. Help me
to see Thy way and take it.
—Dr. E. Stanley Jones
in *Growing Spiritually*

Cancer Is No Respecter of Persons

The phone kept ringing. We were very busy at the clinic. Somehow I became conscious of the ringing of the phone, and I had a premonition that it was an ominous call. A secretary finally answered the phone and told me that my son-in-law, Marion, was on the phone. It was unusual for Marion to call me in the middle of a workday, so I immediately thought, "What's wrong?" The thought raced through my thinking: "He must have some bad news!"

The call from my son-in-law was just that—bad news.

We exchanged the usual pleasantries, and then he said, "I have some bad news. Phyllis has cancer."

I was stunned. I was speechless for a few moments. Shock waves rolled over me. Cancer had attacked my daughter. My reaction was that of a typically overwhelmed father.

It seemed that Phyllis had been having coughing spells and had gone to a good friend, a fine internist, who had X-rayed and made the diagnosis of cancer of the lungs.

I had been through desolate moments and experiences with many of my patients and their families, but I had never had the personal experience of this kind of diagnosis in my own family. This was different.

Are you one of the millions of Americans who is wondering today if you or someone dear to you will soon be one out of the every four Americans who dies from cancer? We don't like to think about that. To do so is to face the unthinkable. We simply cannot comprehend how we would react; moreover, we don't even want to think about it, and so we shove it out of our mind.

But more and more people are having to confront this prospect as the incidence of cancer increases. Cancer is being called today's plague, killing us and our children, our relatives and our friends the way cholera, diphtheria, and smallpox once did. It is virtually epidemic.[1]

When my son-in-law called with that dread news, I asked him for more details. He informed me that they were coming immediately to Houston to go through the tumor and cancer clinic. Her doctor was familiar with the latest procedures being used in research for further development of cancer diagnosis and therapy.

My daughter and her husband were beginning the search that all cancer victims and their families go through. For many it is a search not unlike a puzzling maze. In his search for the right treatment, the cancer patient is often understandably confused. He will read much information on cancer and stumble across both the orthodox and the unorthodox treatments. The very widely publicized and controversial treatment involving the substance called Laetrile will come to his attention. He may discover those who have opted for immunotherapy with good success. Others have taken the natural-food route and claim they have conquered the enemy called cancer. Who is he to believe? What is he to do? And time is always of the essence.

The confusing, intricate network of information gleaned both from reading and in discussion with one's doctor and others leaves the victim and his family more often than not in a state of bewilderment. Added to their confusion is the trauma of knowing that the seriousness of the disease demands a decision. As I have often remarked to my patients, one of the most distressing things about cancer is the fear that evolves in the victims and their loved ones. We fear the unknown. It is a normal reaction.

When I learned of my daughter's cancer, "The Serenity Prayer" that is standard procedure for my patients to read came into my thoughts. I give my patients a copy of this prayer and talk to them about the need to recognize God in their lives. I open the door for them to talk about their inner-most feelings and to express their deep-seated fears. To ignore God at any time in one's life is a foolishness I find difficult to understand; to ignore Him while staring sickness and disease in the face is more than foolish.

We cannot hope to restore the poor health of the body without the power of the God-given metabolic healing mechanism which must function at all times if we are to maintain wellness.

The day I received the distressing call from my son-in-law, I found myself repeating "The Serenity Prayer" as I continued seeing the patients who were scheduled for that day.

> God, grant me the serenity to
> accept the things I cannot change . . .
> Courage to change those things I can,
> and wisdom to know the difference.

I experienced tremendous peace of mind. "The Serenity Prayer" helped me, but it is only one of the many things that can bring peace of mind in the midst of the fear and distress that accompanies the news of cancer, coronary, or any problem one may encounter. (Succeeding pages will point you to resources and things you can do.)

We are a nation of many sick people. We have been defying the laws of God and are reaping the harvest of breaking those laws. God has given us freedom of choice—a choice that many people abuse.

My daughter's condition developed in 1977. She had been working hard, helping her mother-in-law clean up her apartment, which had been flooded. She developed a severe pleurisy pain and began coughing. She went to her local physician, a very fine internist, and he put her on antibiotics and suggested an X-ray. The X-ray indicated that she had a mass. She was immediately hospitalized for additional X-rays and bronchoscopic examination with biopsy. This revealed an "Oat Cell" cancer of the hilum (the opening where vessels enter) of the left lung.

The Houston clinic confirmed the diagnosis and suggested giving chemotherapy in large amounts, and then removing some of her bone marrow, and replacing it if the bone marrow did not regenerate. My son-in-law and I stood by in deep concern. We had decided we would not tell Phyllis what to do; it was her body; it should be her decision.

Phyllis elected not to do this, and I was glad. I felt she would have been another statistic in cancer research. They gave her three to six months to live.

She returned to Kansas City to her own doctor, who instituted some chemotherapy there, and in conference with radiologists decided that it would be well for her to take some radiation therapy. When I was told of this I immediately knew that she would be very sick from the side effects. Radiation sickness is very real and very uncomfortable.

We were on the ragged edge in our concern for Phyllis. Prior to this I had been in touch with a friend, Lyda Livingston, in New York. She had heard what we were doing in the Academy of Preventive Medicine and through the Foundation, and she wanted to learn more. Her interest in preventive medicine developed because of personal experiences, and she was spearheading the development of a rehabilitation center for alcoholics on Long Island in New York. This was an idea that touched a special area with me. I had similar thoughts about developing such an institute where individuals could obtain the benefits of spiritual counsel, psychological help, occupational therapy, and the benefits of a dedicated medical team.

When Lyda Livingston asked me to become a consultant, I quickly agreed. In so doing I became acquainted with a member of the board, Dr. Ron Jones, Director of the Medical Research Institute of the Florida Institute of Technology in Melbourne, Florida. Dr. Jones was very excited about research he had been doing on a product called Palosein, which was a veterinarian medication. It sounded intriguing to me, and I asked him to send me some of his research papers.

I had noticed during the scanning of the research reports that this product, SOD (superoxide dismutase) has been accorded the property of preventing some of the adverse delayed effects of radiation. This sounded very interesting to me because in the field of preventive medicine it was obvious that one of our serious problems was the "zapping" of Americans by man-made radiation, followed by the development of many serious problems from the radiation's damaging effects.

When my daughter's doctor decided that it would be wise to add radiation treatment to the chemotherapy that Phyllis was undergoing, I immediately began to ponder what we could do to prevent the sickness that usually occurs when people are undergoing any type of radiation therapy. I was also thinking about the effects on the healthy cells of the therapy while it was eradicating and slowing down the progress of the wild cells of cancer.

As I gave this serious thought, I asked God for some answers. The pieces then began to fall into place. I knew through Dr. Jones that veterinarians were giving Palosein injections, but I had to discard the idea of using SOD injections, since it wasn't being done on people. Canines were one thing; humans were another.

Still, I was impressed with the need to press this further. I contacted Frank DeLuca, a friend I consider to be a genius researcher, and discussed with him the possibilities of helping my daughter in some way with the product SOD. Of course it was not available in tablet form either. But Frank and I hit upon the solution. He would make it up in liquid form, which she could dilute with distilled water and drop under her tongue.

No More Bad Side-Effects from Radiation

SOD has a short life in its liquid form, and it is best to use it before you receive radiation and shortly afterward. It must be used in close proximity to the time you are exposed to radiation. Phyllis had already had three radiation treatments by the time we got the dilutable solution to her. She had developed a severe esophagitis (inflammation of the passage for food from the pharynx to the stomach). She could not swallow and could not even take medication. It was gratifying to see that in three days after she started on the SOD she had relief from the esophagitis.

I was thrilled beyond words. Not only did I know that the SOD had helped Phyllis, but I sensed that it would benefit mankind. Phyllis had no recurrence of radiation sickness. From what we had learned, we believed also that it would tend to slow down any tendency toward the metastasis (spread of cells) into other areas of the body.

From that point on, Frank DeLuca focused his attention on the properties of SOD and how it could be used on humans. Superoxide dismutase (SOD) is not a new discovery. It was actually isolated in 1938, but its efficacy (power to produce effects or intended results) has only been recently recognized. SOD is a component that can be isolated from animal tissues and from plant sources. It is an enzyme and a relatively stable compound as compared to many other enzymes.

Of course we had placed Phyllis on an overall program that included the taking of protomorphagens (substances made from basic tissues) as well as a microemulsion of A-E and enzymes which has been used effectively in Germany for more than 20 years. Phyllis was on a good nutritional regime and also on what we term ''the cell assurance program,'' which is not only preventive but also therapeutically curative.

A famous philosophy expounds the idea that anything that cures or alleviates symptoms is also preventive in its application. The news of my daughter's lung cancer was terrifying, and it had momentarily devastated me. Many of you reading this book know those feelings, for you have experienced the agony of learning that someone in your family has cancer. Perhaps you yourself have received that dreaded news. Cancer today touches everybody. As one woman who experienced it says, "Either you've got it, or you're scared of getting it."[2]

The American Cancer Society reports that about 53 million Americans now living will eventually have cancer; that is one in four persons according to present rates.[3] Many of you who will have cancer, or will learn that loved ones have this dread disease, can do much to either prevent or postpone it by utilizing the material presented in this book. Beyond that, if it has progressed to the stage where you or someone else cannot be helped physically, the book is still for you. Perhaps you can be instrumental in placing it in someone else's hands so they be spared the agonies that you have endured.

The Most Effective Research

While millions of dollars continue to be poured into cancer research, there are others of us who believe that the most effective research is that done by the individual as he examines his own eating and living habits. In the final analysis, each of us is responsible for his own physical and mental well-being. A growing body of researchers, biochemists, doctors, and laypeople are convinced that a nutritional program based upon preventive measures will drastically alter an individual's chances of getting cancer. Our most devastating disease can be conquered if we are willing to expend the effort to become informed and then act upon what we are learning.

Phyllis was ready and willing to be helped in what many consider non-orthodox ways. She became her own best friend as she listened, read, and learned.

The radiologists were surprised as they noted how much

better Phyllis felt and looked in contrast to most of their patients who were taking radiation treatments. She had begun these treatments in November 1977. In February 1978 she started spitting up blood and then actually was hemorrhaging with her coughing. The doctor was justly fearful that a breakdown of the tumor mass was causing the hemorrhage. Once again she was hospitalized, but X-rays showed very little evidence of the tumor. But minute examination showed that there was still traces of the tumor. In questioning her, the doctor learned that she had been going to art classes; subsequently it was felt that the coughing and bleeding were caused by the ill effects of the fumes from the painting materials. This pointed out to me the deleterious effects of many of what I call the "antinutrition factors" that are in our environment today.

Phyllis Today

In January 1979, Phyllis underwent complete studies with X-rays—bronchoscopic examination with biopsy of the resultant tissues. The pathology report was "scar tissue only." Also, the washings from the secretions in the lung did not show any abnormality. In additon, a complete body scan showed that there was no involvement of the liver, bones, and cerebral tissues. On July 15, 1979, I talked to my daughter on her birthday; she had just undergone another examination which was completely negative for cancer findings.

It is our feeling that the many measures utilized for her case have been beneficial and that she had received the benefits of many procedures which have given such unusual results. These, we believe, can also be employed in the prevention of the chronic degenerative diseases, including cancer.

Can Cancer Be Prevented?

A wise philosopher has written, "The greatest minds are

capable of the greatest vices as well as of the greatest virtues.''

Often a man's love for his vices will overshadow his better judgment. We see this trait in heavy smokers, obese people, and those who disregard the common-sense rules of health and moderation. Dr. Richard A. Passwater, in his important book *Cancer and Its Nutritional Therapies,* in the chapter entitled "Common Sense Ways of Avoiding Cancer," states: ". . . we can prevent much cancer by stopping smoking, occupational safety (or changing jobs), cleaning up the environment and food supply, watching our exposure to sun and X-rays, and proper nutrition and moderation in lifestyle.''[4]

That same belief is expressed by Dr. Ronald J. Glasser in his eloquent book *The Greatest Battle.* Glasser relates that at a national symposium of the ACS (American Cancer Society) in 1976, the audience was astonished to hear that the next 2½ decades will be ''the era of environmental disease, that the majority of all cancers are caused by environmental carcinogens, and that a minimum of 30 to 40 percent of today's malignancies could actually be eliminated by simply applying knowledge already known.''[5]

Can the scourge of cancer be eliminated just as smallpox and polio have been largely overcome? Those involved in the forefront of cancer research are now talking of prevention and not of cures, of control rather than vaccines. This is an encouragement to those of us in the preventive health movement. That throws the burden back onto the individual himself, where it rightly belongs. To expect others to be the guardians of our health is to expect too much.

Since my daughter developed cancer, I have a clearer picture of cancer. For years as a doctor I have been concerned. And I have been willing to stand with those in the forefront calling for preventive measures to combat disease. But when it strikes a family member, something happens. I have read that if we want our children to inherit a sane and healthy world, we must begin taking care of them today. The struggle for their survival is our greatest battle—a struggle no longer against nature, but rather against ourselves.

It is a struggle I have long been committed to, but now there is a new urgency. If by means of this book I can alert and help you, then I shall be forever grateful.

Where have we gone wrong? I am convinced that if we fail to follow God's commands, we have lost our way. We and our children don't have to die before our time. The Bible says that the natural lifespan of an individual is 70 or 80 years (Psalm 90:10). We all know people who have lived well beyond that. There are places in the world today where the people are known to be well into their early hundreds.

What Is the Secret to Defy the Plague of Cancer?

Medical researchers tell us that we humans live approximately 60 years. In the great tradition of medicine and science, physicians and scientists continue to seek new discoveries that will put an end to the suffering and heartache caused by disease. Sometimes the world has been slow to applaud the efforts of such as these; many have gone to their own graves without honor or recognition. It should come as no surprise, therefore, that there are those today who are making discoveries, offering explanations and statements, and suggesting ways to combat cancer—but are being met with outright ridicule.

I am referring more specifically to those who are advocating unorthodox approaches—things anyone can do for himself as a means of drastically cutting one's own chances of having cancer. The day may very well come (all of us are praying it will come very soon) when the breakthrough for the "Big C's"—cancer and coronary—will occur. Then these dread diseases will only be a bad memory, a dark blot on the pages of history. Such a breakthrough may come quite simply, in a growing awareness by people like you that God does have an answer and that He expects you to cooperate with Him and the rules of health that He has set forth.

Exodus 15:26 is frequently quoted as God's promised blessing for the great company of Israelites coming out of

Egypt: "If you will give earnest heed to the voice of the Lord your God, and do what is right in His sight, and give ear to His commandments, and keep all His statutes, I will put none of these diseases upon you which I have put on the Egyptians; for I, the Lord, am your healer" (NASB).

History has shown that the application of these divine instructions made a tremendous impact on countless millions of people. I believe we are long overdue in a return to biblical principles. There is more to believing God than faith; there is practice and the much-overlooked response that He is seeking, called obedience.

FOOTNOTES

1. Dr. Ronald J. Glasser, *The Greatest Battle* (New York: Random House, 1976), p. 3.
2. Mary Beth Moster, *Living with Cancer* (Chicago: Moody Press, 1979), p. 21.
3. *75 Cancer Facts and Figures* (New York: American Cancer Society, 1974), p. 3.
4. Dr. Richard A. Passwater, *Cancer and Its Nutritional Therapies* (New Canaan, Conn.: Keats Publishing Co., 1978), p. 55.
5. Glasser, p. 180.

2

There is little fear of overpopulation in the Western
world—for, with time,
"civilized" countries will be
so decimated by cancer
alone that overpopulation
will not be a problem.
—Dr. Harold W. Harper in
*How You Can Beat the
Killer Diseases*

What Is Cancer?

Science has shown that above all else cancer is a cellular disease. We know that a group of cells growing without proper control is a cancer. Think of cancer cells as a group of anarchists, revolutionaries who begin to do as they please. They begin to sap the body's energy and take all the fuels they want and starve the body's still-healthy cells. Cancer cells cannot change back into normal, healthy cells. These anarchist cells will not cooperate with the rest of the body. They do not want to live under the normal control that exercises its influence on our bodies. Cells that were once friendly and obedient to the powers of the body's control centers take over an area. In the action of their own omnipotent power they assume power and, of course, eventually cause the death of the entire body and their own death as well.

One reason that we must think in terms of primary prevention is the fact that when cells undergo a malignant transformation, they tend to stay that way. As with fanatical revolutionaries of the world in recent years, once these anarchist cells have become alienated and lost their cooperative attitudes, it is impossible to bring them back into normal conditions.

To understand cancer and its companions, we must understand life's basic processes. Cell function is the basis of all life. All tissues, organs, and glands are made up of individual cells. We must think in terms of the cell's activities and how they work together. And we must consider the most important factor in cancer—what controls the cells.

We might also describe the body as a complex and marvelous orchestra with millions of players (cells) all performing together. When the cells are playing in harmony, we get the music of health. When some of them start playing out of tune, we get discord—illness.

It is easy to see that the best way to be healthy is to keep the cells performing in harmony. *Preserving* cellular harmony is much better than struggling to *restore* harmony once the cells have begun their discord. How many times have you heard the old adage, "An ounce of prevention is worth a pound of cure"? Surely the best cure for cancer is not to get it in the first place. This same principle applies to such degenerative diseases as heart attack and diabetes. By the time we get them—by the time they are established—it is often too late.

What shall we do to prevent these dread diseases? First, we must focus on that tiniest player in our physiological orchestra—the cell. Let's consider a *cellular theory of disease*. I call it *hypocellulosis,* a weakness in the cells themselves.

This weakness, *hypocellulosis,* is largely caused by three things: poor genetic patterns, poor nutrition (nutrients we do not take in), and antinutrition (poisons we take in from food, air, and water). The inherent strength of the human cell is directly affected by these factors, and the proper care of the cell itself is the basis for improving health and maintaining the immune processes of the body.

What we have to do to help the body defend itself is to pay attention to the things which reinforce the basic unit of the body, the cell. Now that shouldn't be too difficult to understand.

Poor Genetic Patterns

It pays to have healthy ancestors. But since you and I don't have much choice in the matter, the best thing to do is to keep our cellular system healthy. This means the right amount of the right nutrients at the right time delivered to the right place within our bodies. You can quickly see the problems this poses, for who among us is sure we are doing that 100 percent of the time!

The Psalmist describes how we came into being in beautiful language:

> You made all the delicate, inner parts of my body, and knit them together in my mother's womb. Thank you for making me so wonderfully complex! It is amazing to think about. Your workmanship is marvelous—and how well I know it. You were there while I was being formed in utter seclusion! You saw me before I was born and scheduled each day of my life before I began to breathe. Every day was recorded in your Book!
>
> —Psalm 139:13-16 TLB

What part do inherited genetic traits play in determining one's predisposition to cancer? D.P. Murphy and H. Abbey, writing in *Cancer in Families,* state that certain cancers tend to run in families, for poorly understood reasons. These include cancer of the lung, large bowel, uterus, stomach, and breast, and childhood sarcomas and brain tumors. Your chances of contracting any of these particular cancers seem to be two to four times higher if a close relative has previously developed one of them. The excess risk is restricted to cancers of specific sites; a family history of lung cancer will not predispose to breast cancer.

Familial predisposition to breast cancer is particularly well-established. Sisters or daughters of women who developed breast cancer before menopause are known to be about nine times more likely to get breast cancer than the general population. The risk is still further increased if the relative had cancer in both breasts. Risks for postmenopausal breast cancers are much lower.[1] It is well-known that breast cancer is the leading cause of cancer death among women. It is also known that 95 percent of breast cancers are found by women themselves. At present rates, one out of every 13 American women will develop breast cancer.

It is also known that certain rare cancers or predisposing conditions can be directly inherited. These include multiple polyposis of the colon, which predisposes to colon-rectal cancer, and xeroderma pigmentosum, which predisposes to skin cancer.[2]

Since the healthy body is comprised of colonies of civilized, controlled cells, the process of orderly dividing and redividing is necessary to replenish our body with new cells as old ones die off. Even though many cells are different in appearance and function, these individualistic, functioning cells actually come from the same two cells that joined together in conception.

Researchers now know that the DNA and the nucleus of our cells are the proteins that contain the genetic code. Of course, it is the gene that tells the cell what it will be, how it will act, and how it should act. These controls, which have been basically unchanged for thousands of years, are now the victims of the damaging effects of carcinogens.

A carcinogen is any agent which increases tumor (cancer) induction in man or animals. Knowingly and unknowingly we are exposed to these carcinogens. Carcinogens may affect the cell's genetic material, where they may tie up or simply destroy part of the cell's nucleic acids. In large doses, carcinogens simply kill cells. In smaller doses they poison the cells, causing mutation. Some cells will mutate into unusual shapes and begin duplicating at an unnatural rate. They become cancer cells.

But the problem is not simply the rapid redivision of cells, because our bone marrow manufactures red blood cells fast enough to completely replace all our red blood cells every 120 days. We remake our circulating white cells every six hours. Of course we know that this is not a cancerous process. But a cancerous growth involves *uncontrolled* duplication of *unnatural* cells.

"Cancer Is Killing Kids" is a chapter title in the book *Cancer Facts and Fallacies*, by J.I. Rodale & Staff. This tells us that we need to sound the warning to pregnant women to be very conscientious about what they put into their bodies during pregnancy. The authors ask the question, "Can the fact that more children are contracting cancer be one of the still-unknown effects of the myriad potent chemicals we are forced to combine in our bodies with no knowledge of what they combine into, or what they do to us?"[3]

Go slow on additives in your diet, mothers, and particularly if you are pregnant! Children can grow up grateful if their mothers didn't smoke while carrying them. Dr. W.J. McCormick wrote in the *Journal of Applied Nutrition* (volume 14, Nos. 1, 2) of his conviction that smoking by pregnant women is a factor in the rising rate of leukemia in children. In support of his contention, Dr. McCormick quoted two cancer workers, Lawrence and Donland *(Cancer Research,* 12:900-904, December 1952): ". . . the acute leukemias are an example of disease that may have such an origin [embryonic tissue damaged by carcinogenic agents]. Leukemia seems to be increasing in recent years, especially in children under five years, suggestively due to carcinogenic stimulation in prenatal life.[4]

Another warning for the expectant mother relates to submitting to X-rays, especially in the pelvic area, either for treatment or diagnosis, unless there is a medical reason so urgent that waiting until the birth of the child is not practical. Much evidence has been published in medical journals showing the link between leukemia in children (as well as other congenital defects in newborn babies) and prenatal use of radiation.[5]

The picture this paints is grim, but leukemia and any form of cancer is terrible, so shielding readers from the truth is not doing anyone a favor. The preventive answer is to studiously avoid any unnecessary radiation, and then to supplement one's diet with therapeutic augmentation of concentrated nutrients. It is especially important to maintain a high level of vitamin C in the system, and to eliminate as many processed foods as possible.

The warning needs to be sounded and repeated of the dangers of taking drugs during pregnancy. Not only can these drugs be cancer-producing, but they can and do cause gross physical congenital defects. If drugs can cause arms not to grow and can produce other deformities, who is to say what these drugs are doing to the subtler and more-difficult-to-evaluate effects on a developing child's personality, intelligence, motor coordination, and psychological growth? Almost everyone will recall the thalidomide tragedies of a number of years ago. Dilantin is another drug which has proven to cause facial malformations in children. Fetal cells can be injured by these and other drugs and can cause congenital defects.[6] What is a medication for the mother becomes a poison for the infant.

So what is cancer? The cancers diagnosed today did not break out yesterday or even the day before, but started many years ago when the body lost its inherent ability to control cell reduplication.

If a body is subjected to very small doses of radiation or carcinogens, less than the amount that is needed to kill the cells, there will be some cells that will eventually become anarchists, able to grow without control, assuming unusual shapes and beginning to reduplicate at unnatural rates. Eventually they will overcome all of the tissues that surround that colony of anarchists. Then they will begin to take off from this and go to other areas to start their revolutionary processes. At that stage the doctor will tell you that the cancer has invaded distant tissues, and you will hear the word *metastasis.*

Metastasis means a passing over, a transition. In medicine this refers to the shifting of disease from one part or organ of the body to another unrelated to it, as by the transfer of pathogenic (the production or development of a disease) organisms or of the cells of a malignant tumor.

It is safe to say that carcinogenic agents are like a time bomb that will eventually explode and destroy our bodies. Researcher Isaac Berenblum already in the 1940s gave us some information which was a tremendous advance in understanding cancer. He proved that even infinitesimal continued damage and exposure to normal cells by carcinogenic (cancer-causing) chemicals will eventually cause a malignant condition. His experiments pointed out that even very minute contact with carcinogens would cause a premalignant state that would lead to malignant conditions later.

Now I ask you, who among us hasn't been and isn't being exposed to carcinogens daily? Why then do some people develop cancer while others do not? It must have something to do with one's cells. It must also have something to do with what is going into one's body, and the individual's ability to assimilate that intake. This brings up a factor called metabolic balance, discussed later in this book.

Good health is necessary to protect the body against these abnormal cell functions, which lead to premature, chronic, degenerative diseases. God's answer is to *prevent it!*

Preventive medicine places responsibility on the person who understands these facts and is willing to do what is necessary to preserve his health. It involves adopting a healthy lifestyle for the whole person. For this reason it is frequently called holistic or wholistic health care, which simply means *wholeness* and completeness—becoming well and staying well in body, mind, and spirit.

Poor Nutrition

One of the great tragedies of modern medicine is that not enough physicians are paying attention to what their patients are putting into their mouths. Little thought is given to informing the patient of the health-giving qualities of a well-functioning gastrointestinal tract.

There are some doctors who should go back to what I call
"alimentary school," for they have overlooked the effect on
the entire body of breakdowns of the body's ability to
assimilate and utilize the things we put into our mouths. Not
only must the body break down and assimilate the smallest
and finest components of food, but it must also be capable of
using it at the cellular level. And the biological cleanup crew
must empty trillions of "wastebaskets" and "garbage pails"
every day. When these functions break down within our
bodies, the advent of such degenerative diseases as cancer,
heart disease, and diabetes are much more likely.

Thus we cannot afford to wait and hope for a miracle
cancer cure. We have everything to gain and nothing
whatever to lose by initiating a plan to maintain the good
health of our cells.

The pollution of air, food, and water seriously affects our
cellular function because the liver cannot detoxify (throw out
the poisons) coming from the additives in our food and the
unnatural chemicals in our environment. Over a prolonged
period of time (which will vary according to the individual's
cellular capacity to withstand the assaults being made upon
it), weakened by poor nutrition, struggling with pollutants,
the cells get sick and we have sick tissues, glands, and vital
organs.

The condition of a generalized overall inclusive malnutrition state, which I call *anutrientosis,* is nearly universal
among Americans due to the devitalizing and overprocessing
of our food and the elimination of vital nutrients. Resistance
by the normal tissues is nature's way of dealing with the
cancer process. Cancer prevention consists of keeping the
body healthy enough for its immune system to eliminate abnormal cellular growths as soon as they appear. To do this requires, among other things, that we stay away from those
things that we know damage normal cells and start abnormal
cellular growth.

Instructions for optimum health were laid down for us in

the Bible. There is no denying that, for they are in the first chapter of Genesis:

> Behold, I have given you every plant yielding seed that is on the surface of all the earth, and every tree which has fruit yielding seed; it shall be food for you . . . and to every thing that moves on the earth which has life, I have given every green plant for food (vv. 29, 30, NASB).

This is God speaking to the first man and woman who inhabited the earth.

> And God saw all that He had made, and behold, it was very good (v. 31 NASB).

It was good for them then, and it should be good for us now. But is it always good? Has our tampering with nature helped or hindered?

The refined foods which constitute so much of the diet of Americans is not as ''refined''—wholesome and of superior quality—as one might suppose. In fact, quite the opposite is true. From 50 to 90 percent of various nutrients are lost when we eat refined bread. Some people say, "The whiter the bread the better," to which I would reply, "The whiter the bread the sooner you're dead!"

Much of the necessary fiber we need in our diets is lost through this process of refining. Even so-called "enriched" bread loses about 70 percent of its fiber content. Low-fiber foods go through the intestinal tract much slower than high-fiber foods. On a high-fiber diet, foods go through in about 30 to 36 hours, but it may take more than 80 hours for the food to go through the intestinal tract on a low-fiber diet. Can you see the danger this poses? If we have cancer-producing substances in our diet, and this food lies in the intestinal tract a longer period of time, there is a much greater possibility of developing cancer of the colon.

So not only are we eating food lacking in nutritive elements, but they are also lacking in fiber.

Which is better for you, a whole orange or drinking the orange juice? And how few today are even squeezing and making their own fresh juice! Instead, they are substituting canned or frozen juices. But if you want to add fiber to your diet, you will eat the whole orange.

Go through a typical day's diet for the average family and you will soon recognize how many vital nutrients are not taken in. Most of us consume more than our weight in what is often called empty calories each year. I call them "sickness-breeding calories."

Studies show that teenagers are developing cirrhosis of the liver. Why? Overconsumption of soft drinks is a contributing factor.

Hidden sources of sugar exist in much of our diet (mayonnaise or salad dressings, refined cereals, the soft drinks mentioned above, jams and jellies, ice cream, pies and other rich desserts, juices, ad infinitum). Sugar decreases our ability to destroy bacteria. Cancer cells thrive on glucose, and glucose is sugar. If you eat 18 to 20 teaspoons of sugar on an empty stomach, within one hour your ability to destroy bacteria is decreased about 50 percent. Do you think you don't eat that many spoonsful? The average individual consumes 34 teaspoons a day in one form or another, mostly hidden.

Then there are the additives which contribute to nutritional problems. The fighting mechanism in our bodies becomes less effective in warding off those substances which are contributing to disease. The toxins released into our systems cause a breakdown in our cellular structure. Dr. Art Ulene, NBC's *Today* show doctor, in his book *Feeling Fine,* poses the question, "if food manufacturers decided to remove all the additives mixed into their products at the rate of one a day, how long would it take before all products were free of additives?" He answers that by writing, "About fourteen years, because an estimated 5000 additives are in use!"

Eating the foods God said were "very good"—fruits, vegetables, nuts, whole-grain cereals, legumes, beans, peas—provides a bacterial flora that is more aerobic (free oxygen is present).

What is generally not known by the average person is that cancer cells have to have a lot of their kind of energy—the nonoxygen kind—in order to live. And it takes a long time for this energy to build up. That's why there is a long latency period for some cancers to develop. So people who are not eating well enough to use the oxygen energy cycle will have a buildup of deficient cells. Is it any wonder that God told us to eat nature's way? To do so is to insure for our cells an oxygen energy pathway where disease cannot thrive.

The average housewife is the target of intensive advertising and propaganda designed to seduce her into believing that crusaders for better health are crazy. The consumer public has long been duped. "She has been flattered into thinking she knows all about nutrition while, in truth, she has been kept in relative ignorance about the shortcomings of the highly refined, chemically treated devitalized foods she feeds her family; she has been given a false sense of security that she is protected by the nation's food laws. She has been indoctrinated with false information about what constitutes good foods. Generally, she does not know that it is possible to be overfed and undernourished at the same time.[7]

The problem with eating even many fruits and vegetables bought in the typical grocery store is that so many of them are sprayed with poisonous chemicals, fruits are picked green and dyes applied, and the consumer can never be quite sure that she is really getting what she is seeking.

Every poison taken into the body, if it cannot be excreted rapidly in its original state, must be detoxified. This places a heavy and continuing burden on the liver and various other organs. In the process of detoxification certain vitamins are used up, primarily the B vitamins and vitamin C. The detoxifying organs, in order to get the extra vitamins necessary to do the extra work demanded of them, take vitamins from other parts of the body. This can cause a vitamin deficiency. Eventually it can set off a chain reaction; certain organs may break down from this burden and become unable to do their job, which leads to serious ailments, degenerative diseases including cancer, and even death.

Considering how many of our foods are lacking in vital nutrients, is it any wonder that we have a cancer epidemic in this country today? We are reaping the results of what has been sown for years. Cancer is the condition of cellular crisis.

A myth has long existed in this country—a myth that says we are the healthiest people on the face of the earth and that we live longer than other peoples. This myth that says we are the best-fed nation has been perpetuated by the food industry at the expense of our health.

The average American eats only a small percentage of the nutrient-containing foods necessary to sustain health and a normal sugar-regulating mechanism. A western university recently compiled ''the most popular adult diet in the United States.'' Examine the sample menu shown below that was derived from this diet; it illustrates the gross imbalance, in most American diets, in favor of useless starches and away from nutrients and proteins. Then compare this diet with the sample 2000-calorie Nutrition-Wise Daily Menu. The tables that follow these menus show the nutrient totals of the most popular U.S. diet and those of the 2000-calorie Nutrition-Wise daily menu and how each compares percentagewise with the U.S. Government recommended dietary allowance (RDA).

MOST POPULAR ADULT DIET IN THE UNITED STATES

	Carbo-hydrates	Protein	Fat	Total
	Calories			
Breakfast				
Coffee and donuts (cream and sugar)	160	20	150	330

	Carbo-hydrates	Protein	Fat	Total
	Calories			
Snacks				
Coffee and sweet roll (cream and sugar)	140	25	70	235
Lunch				
2 hot dogs	10	60	180	250
Pickles	10	5	5	20
Soft drink	80	0	0	80
Apple Pie (small slice)	210	10	115	335
Snack				
Coffee and sweet roll (cream and sugar)	140	25	50	215
Dinner				
Meatballs (3 small)	45	50	175	270
Spaghetti (1 cup)	175	30	10	215
Green beans (½ cup)	10	5	0	15
Chopped salad	25	10	5	40
Chocolate cake	75	5	30	110
French Bread	60	5	5	70
Late Snack				
Coffee (cream and sugar)	20	0	25	45
Cookies (2)	150	10	60	220
TOTAL	1,310 (51%)	260 (11%)	880 (38%)	2,450

2000-CALORIE NUTRITION-WISE MENU

	Carbo-hydrates	Protein	Fat	Total
Breakfast				
3 apricot halves, stewed (noncalorically sweetened)	55	5	—	60
½ cup rice, cooked, (whole grain)	85	10	—	95
1 egg plus 1 egg white, scrambled with	—	40	50	90
1 tbsp. nonfat dry milk solids	15	10	—	25
1 tbsp. wheat germ	10	5	—	15
2 tbsp. water	—	—	—	—
¼ tsp. brewer's yeast	—	—	—	—
3 oz. dried or chipped beef	—	115	50	165
1 slice whole-wheat bread	45	10	5	60
1 tsp. butter or margarine	—	—	35	35
1 glass (8 oz.) skim milk	50	35	—	85
TOTALS	260	230	140	630

	Carbo-hydrates	Protein	Fat	Total
Lunch				
1 cup consomme	—	35	—	35
1 envelope unflavored gelatin	—	30	—	30
6 oz. white fish, broiled	—	160	20	180
½ cup mustard greens	10	5	—	15
1 hard-cooked egg white	—	15	—	15
½ cup lima beans with pimento	65	20	—	85
1 slice whole-wheat bread	45	10	5	60
Lemon pudding	40	20	40	100
1 glass (8 oz.) skim milk	50	35	—	85
TOTALS	210	330	65	605
Dinner				
Salad: 1 med. tomato, stuffed with ½ cup				
cottage cheese and	25	5	5	35
1 tsp. chopped parsley	10	90	5	105
New England Boiled Dinner	75	165	105	345
Celery sticks (¼ stalk)	5	—	—	5
1 slice whole-wheat bread	45	10	5	60
Dessert: Molded fruit salad, made with				
1 envelope gelatin (unflavored)	—	30	—	30
¾ cup water	—	—	—	—
2 tbsp. lemon juice	10	—	—	10
½ cup fruit cocktail, noncalorically				
sweetened	45	—	—	45
1 glass (8 oz.) skim milk	50	35	—	85
TOTALS	265	335	120	720
Before Bedtime				
½ glass (4 oz.) skim milk	25	20	—	45
TOTALS	760 (38%)	915 (45%)	325 (16%)	2,000

RECOMMENDED DIETARY ALLOWANCE BASED ON ADULT MALE 154 POUNDS
2800 Total Daily Calories

Calcium	Phosphorus	Iron	Sodium	Potassium	A	B_1	B_2	Niacin	C	D
800 mg.	800 mg.	10 mg.	—	—	5000 IU	1.4 mg.	1.7 mg.	18 mg.	60 mg.	—

MOST POPULAR ADULT DIET IN THE UNITED STATES
2450 Total Daily Calories

Calcium	Phosphorus	Iron	Sodium	Potassium	A	B_1	B_2	Niacin	C	D
487 mg.	1185 mg.	13.6 mg.	3605 mg.	1452 mg.	2400 mg.	0.90 mg.	1.44 mg.	16.94 mg.	trace	trace

PERCENTAGE OF RECOMMENDED DIETARY ALLOWANCE IN MOST POPULAR ADULT DIET

Calcium	Phosphorus	Iron	Sodium	Potassium	A	B_1	B_2	Niacin	C	D
60%	145%	136%	—	—	40%	60%	80%	90%	—	—

NUTRITION-WISE MENU
2000 Total Daily Calories

Calcium	Phosphorus	Iron	Sodium	Potassium	A	B_1	B_2	Niacin	C	D
2165 mg.	3475 mg.	30.3 mg.	8600 mg.	6015 mg.	14,195 IU	462 mg.	23.40 mg.	102.31	195 mg.	85 IU

PERCENTAGE OF RECOMMENDED DIETARY ALLOWANCE IN NUTRITION-WISE MENU

Calcium	Phosphorus	Iron	Sodium	Potassium	A	B_1	B_2	Niacin	C	D
270%	435%	300%	—	—	280%	330%	135%	565%	320%	—

NOTE: — indicates no available information from RDA

You can see that the Nutrition-Wise program is high in protein and essential nutrients and low in carbohydrates and fat. And while the recommended dietary allowance totals might sustain an American on a day-to-day basis, they are hardly enough to restore a state of metabolic equilibrium and a feeling of peak energy after years of bad eating and functional breakdown.

Dr. Jean Mayer of Harvard's Department of Nutrition and Chairman of the 1969 White House Conference reported in *Science* (April 21, 1972): "Malnutrition, whether caused by poverty or improper diet, contributes to the alarming health situation in the United States today."

Perhaps it is difficult for you to understand why this country has such poor nutrition with its abundance of foodstuffs. The answer lies in food processing, the fact that nutrients are lost during storage and shipping of food, and that food-quality factors decrease with time. Some nutrients are destroyed by oxygen in the air (especially vitamin E); others evaporate during normal drying; and exposure to light and heat also breaks up the sensitive vitamin molecules. So even though a conscientious homemaker may set before her family a beautifully prepared meal, it may be sadly lacking in vital nutrients. Here are some examples (taken from Dr. Passwater's book):

Peas cooked garden-fresh lose 56 percent of their vitamins by the time they are served; but canned peas lose 94 percent, and frozen peas lose 83 percent.

Canned:
30 percent in the scalding process
25 percent in the sterilization process
27 percent in the liquor diffusion
12 percent in reheating
_____
94 percent total

Frozen:
25 percent in the scalding process
19 percent in the freezing process
15 percent in the thawing process
24 percent in cooking
_____
83 percent total

It is important to remember that fresh foods lose their nutrients rapidly because of enzymatic decomposition. Few of us grow our own fruits and vegetables. We must rely on our markets. Refrigeration helps, but it does not eliminate the problem. Ideally, we should all grow our own food products like our forefathers were required to do. Garden-fresh vegetables are known to contain nearly twice the vitamin C, for example, of market-fresh vegetables (according to U.S. Agriculture Department Handbook No. 8).

What do the Eskimos of the Arctic, the Hunzakuts of northeast Pakistan, certain tribes in Nigeria, the Vilcabamba Indians of Ecuador, the Abkhasians of the Soviet Union, the nonurban populations in Southeast Asia, and the Hopi and Navajo Indians in the United States have in common? Laetrile researchers tell us it has everything to do with their diet and their considerable ingestion of vitamin B17 through the foods they eat. Those Hopi and Navajo Indians in this country who adhere to the diets of their forefathers have demonstrated that even in this country we can escape the clutches of the "Big C"—cancer. Recent studies of Seventh-Day Adventists in this country also reflect a B17 component in their mostly vegetarian diet.[8]

In speaking before the Senate Select Committee on Nutrition and Human Needs (on June 19-21, 1974), I stated: "Centuries of observation have taught us that humans get sick on poor-quality foods and stay healthy when they eat foods endowed with proper nutritional content, just as plants and animals do."

It is generally acknowledged by theologians and Bible believers that the laws of God recorded in the Hebrew Scriptures can be classified into three categories: the moral law (summed up in the Ten Commandments); the dietary law (Leviticus 11 and Deuteronomy 14:3-21); and the ceremonial law (Exodus 25 through 40 and the book of Leviticus). There are those who contend that the dietary law was only meant for Israel. It seems unwise to me that we should reject the dietary law and insist that the Ten Commandments are meant for all.

Both were given at the same time and on the same level. We have broken the dietary laws God established and are reaping the harvest of our foolishness.

Antinutrition

Dr. Harold W. Harper, writing in *How You Can Beat the Killer Diseases,* maintains that there is a "raging pandemicity of cancer in the 'civilized' Western world—one in which pollutants, contaminants, and poisons abound in the air, water, and food we consume, while at the same time we have virtually removed our natural defense against cancer from our food supply."[9]

The enormous increase of cancer, particularly in the last decade, can be laid at the feet of environmental influences to which cellular respiration is subjected. This cumulative poisoning takes its toll. The great Law of Life is replenishment. The body needs to be constantly supplied with the elements of which it is composed. Failure to do this will result in disease in one form or another and eventual death. But even though we may be eating abundantly, as has been pointed out, a diet consisting wholly or mostly of devitalized foods will result in a breaking down of our cells. This combined with the poisons we ingest result in what I call *antinutrition.*

The world in which we live is actually quite hostile to human health. A flight to the country from the city is more difficult to achieve these days. And, once there, it is not unusual to find that the polluted city air has reached the country spaces too. The poisons of modern living are insidious; it takes a special determination to seek ways to improve the quality of one's living in order to actually achieve some quantity of life.

We do have it much easier and better in almost every aspect of living than our fathers, grandfathers, and great-grandfathers. They faced perils, but so do we of a different nature. Our scientific advances, skills, and genius have unleashed into the atmosphere killing pollutants which ultimately may mean that they (along with nuclear facilities) will stand to inherit the earth rather than people.

Australian-born and-educated, Dr. Helen Caldicott is an environmental activist and now a permanent resident of the United States. She states in her enlightening book *Nuclear Madness,* "I contend that nuclear technology threatens life on our planet with extinction. If present trends continue, the air we breathe, the food we eat, and the water we drink will soon be contaminated with enough radioactive pollutants to pose a potential health hazard far greater than any plague humanity has ever experienced. Unknowingly exposed to these radioactive poisons, some of us may be developing cancer right now. Others may be passing damaged genes, the basic chemical units which transmit hereditary characteristics, to future generations. And more of us will inevitably be affected unless we bring about a drastic reversal of our government's pronuclear policies."[10]

To read material like this is to become aware of the radioactive contaminants polluting our planet and the implications of this to us individually. The very survival of our species depends on individual concern. Daily we are exposed to unacceptable risks to health and life caused by technologies which, according to Dr. Caldicott and other voices being raised like hers, propagate suffering, disease, and death. The significance of SOD, which I gave to my daughter Phyllis, comes into better focus since it prevents the side effects of radiation.

The truth is that we as a nation are courting catastrophe. But not we alone; "By making 'peaceful' nuclear technology available to any nation wealthy enough to buy a nuclear reactor, we are inviting other countries to join the international 'nuclear club' militarily, as well as economically."[11]

The tragedy is that most of us live our lives in seemingly normal ways, unaware of the silent threat to our health and our hopes for future generations. "It can't happen to us" or

"It won't happen to us" would be the answer many of us would give if confronted with the facts. Apathy—a pathetic indifference, a "so what" attitude—is all too common. "Eat, drink, and be merry, for tomorrow you may die," may be an old saw, but it's very much alive and a current assessment of our American scene.

We live in a society accustomed, for the most part, to immediate self-gratification. "Get while the getting's good" is the unwritten maxim which many have subscribed to for themselves and their families. We have geared ourselves to think in terms of short-term satisfaction in hopes of finding happiness. That "happiness," so-called, wears thin while staring death in the face. And death is the enemy that everyone eventually faces both for himself and loved ones.

But we are death-deniers. We delude ourselves and allow others to mesmerize us into thinking that those who protest about pollutants, the dangers of nuclear power, and what we call public-health hazards are quacks and flag-carrying zealots.

You can't measure the value of human life in dollars when your own life, or that of your husband, wife, or children, is at stake. "Nuclear power and nuclear war are primarily medical issues. Arguments about profits, jobs, and politics are reduced to irrelevancy when our children are threatened with epidemics of leukemia, cancer, and inherited disease. . . .

"It is currently believed that 80 percent of all cancers are caused by environmental factors. By definition, therefore, they are preventable. The U.S. government spends millions of dollars each year funding medical research into the cause and cure of this dreaded disease. At the same time, however, it spends billions funding the weapons and nuclear power industries which propagate the diseases doctors are struggling to conquer. We in the medical profession must begin to practice what I call 'Political medicine,' something we are not trained to do. Political medicine opposes industrial practices which contaminate the environment with disease-causing agents. In this way it attempts to attack the 'front end' of the cancer cycle and prevent the disorder from occurring, rather than trying to cure malignancies after they are diagnosed, when it is often too late."[12]

We live in a polluted world. You cannot hope to escape unscathed. What then is the answer? An awakening from our false sense of security is first of all in order. An aroused public conscience can do much to bring about change. Then we must individually assume responsibility for what we eat and drink, and for our manner of living.

Back to the title of this chapter. What is cancer? To answer that we have to go back to the book of beginnings in the Bible. Not everyone chooses to accept the Genesis account, but we do, and this forms the basis for our understanding of sickness and death.

In the beginning God created a planet called Earth that was formless and void. As the Spirit of God moved over the surface of the earth the spectacular events of further creation took place. After each major creative event the Bible records that God looked upon it and "saw that it was good."

The first time the Bible records that something was "not good" was when God looked upon the first man He had made and saw him in his aloneness and decided to "make him a helper suitable for him" (Genesis 2:18 NASB).

Paradise Ruined

To have walked with the Spirit of God in the perfection of paradise on earth must have been joy unequaled. Only Adam and Eve knew the moral purity that would enable them to have that kind of fellowship with the Creator of the universe.

Adam and Eve were told by God what to do. The prohibition which God placed upon them shows the importance that God attached to food.

> The Lord God planted all sorts of beautiful trees there in
> the garden, trees producing the choicest of fruit. At the center

of the garden he placed the Tree of Life, and also the Tree of Conscience, giving knowledge of Good and Bad. A river from the land of Eden flowed through the garden to water it. . . .

The Lord God placed the man in the Garden of Eden as its gardener, to tend and care for it. But the Lord God gave the man this warning: "You may eat any fruit in the garden except fruit from the Tree of Conscience—for this fruit will open your eyes to make you aware of right and wrong, good and bad. If you eat its fruit, you will be doomed to die."

—(Genesis 2:9, 10, 15-17 TLB)

An innocent stroll took place in the beautiful garden followed by a confrontation with the crafty serpent, disobedience, and the great fall into sin and suffering resulted. This was the turning point in man's destiny, and we have been the inheritors of a sin-scarred earth.

We overlook something that God said to Adam and Eve. He told them they could know what is right and what is wrong. And we have that inherent ability as well. Wrong choices, a disregard for common-sense rules of right living— these things contribute not only to a polluted world but to self-pollution.

Cancer is cells gone awry. Damaged cells lead to all of man's diseases.

A body is made up of billions of normal cells, all of which multiply and divide in an orderly manner to perform their own particular functions. Whenever these cells, for some as-yet-unknown reason, go berserk and grow in a disorderly and chaotic manner, crowding out normal cells and robbing them of nourishment, the condition is known as cancer.[13]

The growth of these abnormal cells is usually insidious and unnoticed until it reaches an advanced stage where there is pain or other symptoms (many of which we ignore in the early stages).

Is There Any Hope?

Yes, there is hope. God's laws are God's preventive grace. Health was God's will for Adam and Eve, and God hasn't changed His mind for you and me. We can possess radiant health and live a long, disease-free life. There are some rules to be obeyed, some things to do, and some things not to do.

The Spirit in Trouble

Dr. E. Stanley Jones, powerful theologian and religion writer, tells us the Japanese have a word for sickness: "the spirit in trouble." Dr. Jones states that "Very often it is the 'spirit in trouble' that produces illness." As this wise man reminds us, we need to come to God and find the source of getting the spirit out of trouble. Therein lies our hope.

FOOTNOTES

1. Samuel S. Epstein, M.D., *The Politics of Cancer* (San Francisco: Sierra Club Books, 1978), pp. 460, 461.
2. Ibid., p. 461.
3. J.I. Rodale & Staff, *Cancer Facts and Fallacies* (Emmaus, Penna.: Rodale Books Inc., 1969), p. 64.
4. Ibid., p. 40.
5. Ibid., pp. 41, 42.
6. Dr. Ronald J. Glasser, *The Greatest Battle* (New York: Random House, 1976), Chapter V, "Old Plagues and Old Warnings."
7. William Longgood, *The Poisons in Your Food* (New York: Pyramid Books, 1960, 1969), p. 23.
8. Harold W. Harper, M.D., and Michael L. Culbert, *How You Can Beat the Killer Diseases* (New Rochelle, N.Y.: Arlington House, 1977), pp. 157, 158.
9. Ibid., p. 162.
10. Dr. Helen Caldicott, *Nuclear Madness* (Brookline, Mass.: Autumn Press, Inc., 1978), p. 15.
11. Ibid., p. 17.
12. Ibid., pp. 88, 89.
13. *Everything You Always Wanted to Know About Cancer But Were Afraid to Ask* (n.p.: United Cancer Council, n.d.), p. 3.

3

Eighty to ninety percent of
cancer in the world is
caused by: 1. What we
breathe; 2. What we
drink; 3. What we eat,
and 4. Radiation in our environment.
—The World Health
Organization

Why Cancer?

We are all exposed to agents that cause cancer. It is unavoidable—in the air we breathe, the water we drink, the food we eat, and the effects of radiation in our environment.

Hippocrates was right! Hippocrates, you may recall, was that ancient Greek physician who has been accurately called "The Father of Medicine." The Hippocratic oath is generally taken by students receiving the M.D. degree. It is attributed to Hippocrates and regarded as setting forth an ethical code for the medical profession today. If Hippocrates could see what is happening in the world today, and the hazards to which human life is exposed, as we facetiously say, he would probably turn over in his grave. Hippocrates stated:

> . . . it appears to me necessary to every physician to be skilled in nature, and to strive to know, if he would wish to perform his duties, what a man is in relation to the articles of food and drink, and to his other occupations, and what are the effects of each of them to every one.
>
> Whoever does not know what effect these things produce upon a man cannot know the consequences which result from them.

> Whoever pays no attention to these things, or paying attention, does not comprehend them, how can he understand the diseases which befall a man? For, by every one of these things a man is affected and charged this way and that, and the whole of his life is subjected to them, whether in health, convalescence, or disease. Nothing else, then, can be more important or more necessary to know than these things.

It was Hippocrates who first identified cancer around 400 B.C. We are told that he divided tumors into two classifications: the "innocuous" or benign, and "dangerous" or malignant. The word *cancer* itself is derived from the Latin word for "crab," *cancrum*. It was Hippocrates' word choice for "dangerous" tumors.

The World Health Organization has pointed out that 80 to 90 percent of cancer is caused by 1) what we breathe, 2) what we drink, 3) what we eat, and 4) radiation in our environment. A look at these four things in closer perspective is in order as we try to gain an understanding of the *why* of cancer.

What We Breathe

As one might suspect, cancer is twice as prevalent in urban areas where there is high air pollution. A Los Angeles survey showed death rates (from all causes) as 27.3 in high-carbon-monoxide and high-pollution areas compared to 19.1 in low-pollution areas. Laboratory studies show that the incidence of cancer rises 5 percent with each additional microgram of benzo (a) pyrene found in 1000 cubic meters of air. (A microgram equals only 1/30 millionth of an ounce.)

The air we breathe carries a myriad of hazardous substances. Sulfur dioxide, an acknowledged cause of cancer, is a result of burning low-grade fuel oil and exhausts into the air. The heavy metal cadmium is released from copper and zinc refining. More than 200 million tons of pollutants are dumped into the atmosphere each year, primarily from the internal combustion engine; and 94 million tons of carbon monoxide are in the air, primarily from automobiles.

Acroleonin comes from diesel exhausts, parathion from insecticides, and petro- and organically-based matter from herbicides. To compound the problem, deadly ozones are synthesized under the sun's rays as all these chemicals interact in the atmosphere.

It is a wind of illness that we breathe.

Nor is it probably any better indoors, in the home or office, wherever you might work. There are over 300,000 toxic or potentially toxic brand-name consumer products available to the home—aerosols, cosmetics, cleaners, pesticides, drugs, and other trappings of our modern life. Not much is known of their pollutant potential, alone or in combinations with each other. As an example, certain cleaning products when mixed with vinegar create the deadly chlorine gas of the type that killed thousands during World War I.

Awareness of pollution is quite universal. Newspaper and magazine headlines have screamed at us about it for some time. Most of us know the discomforting effects of pollution on an especially bad day when, for one reason or another, the air seems so grimy you can almost taste it. You are brought up short in your thinking when the thought flashes through your head, "I'm actually having to breathe this stuff!"

Air pollution, however, is subtle and disguised. Many modern-day ailments baffle the attending physician. Allergy and sinus troubles plague all-too-many people. Often the doctor has to acknowledge that these and other problems are of an unknown cause. Sometimes they will label them psychosomatic (meaning there is no identifiable inciting physical cause or causes). No one will deny that some illnesses are indeed caused by psychic or social stresses. But hundreds of doctors are now readily admitting that a truly surprising number of ailments stem from exposure to our polluted environment.

And that's pretty scary.

Is it any wonder that many researchers, especially those in the health field, are insisting that cancer is a disease of civilization unknown in healthful-living primitive areas? Is it any wonder that the incidence of cancer has skyrocketed to such unbelievable proportions, with most of us living today having been exposed to environmental causes and industrial pollutants in the atmosphere much of our lives? This was not necessarily true for our grandparents, and it was certainly far less true for our great-grandparents.

Scientists now agree that most adult malignancies have their beginning in childhood, adolescence, and early adult life, with some beginning even before birth. Anything that strikes one out of every four Americans and two out of every three families has to be considered as having a fairly common root cause. What could that possibly be, other than the air we breathe, the foods we eat, and the water we drink? Certainly it is true that there are many unknowns in the causes of cancer, but it is equally true that enough is known so that even the medical profession is now agreeing that 75 to 85 percent of all cancers have nothing to do with viruses or even genetics, and that they do not develop from trauma or because of infections, but that they result from exposure to environmental causes and industrial pollutants.[2]

Statistics are saddening. This modern scourge (with which cold hard facts confront us) tells us unmistakably that the things that mean so much to us and our present-day standard of living—these very things that we take so much for granted and without which we would feel that we were living back in the dark ages—it is these that are contributing to our cancer epidemic. Walk through your house and your garage. What would you be willing to eliminate? Go outside, look up into the sky, and watch that beautiful plane glide through the sky. You can see the ''bird,'' but you can't always see the contaminants it leaves in the atmosphere as it gracefully wings its way from coast to coast. I repeat, that's scary. What would we do without air travel in the world today!

One cannot always explain the sudden headache, the nasal problems that come on unawares, the nausea and other peculiar symptoms that flare up unbidden and always unwelcome. Whether it is indoor or outdoor pollutants, fumes from cars, buses, or trucks, or the gas range in one's kitchen, pollutants are pollutants are pollutants. And most of us love the sources of our pollution.

Many instances could be cited of actual cities where it has been proven that certain industries are polluting the environment, playing havoc with our health, and shortening our lives—yet efforts to remedy the situation, to move the offenders, are fought tooth and nail. We are dollar-conscious to such an extent that we'd rather suffer physically and take our chances than give up that which would affect our pocketbooks. These industries provide good employment for thousands of people. Wages are high and working conditions are generally acceptable and even pleasant. To move these industries into less-densely populated areas would greatly affect the economy almost nationwide. And even with such moves, employees would still be needed to work. This is a dilemma not easily solved.

Creature comforts mean more than life itself. Our excessive use of energy throws tons of pollutants into the air. Rather than change our ways, we lethargically yawn in the face of the facts. Still later, we will be crying at the bedside of afflicted loved ones.

Insomnia, anxiety, fatigue, manic behavior, amnesia, and even schizophrenia can be traced in some instances to polluters in the home. Gas appliances in particular are known offenders. The hazards in our homes no longer make home a safe refuge. Even the cosmetics commonly in use may, over an extended period of time, contribute to irritation and in some cases severe infections, open wounds, or skin cancers. Chemical reactions between particular cosmetics and the ultraviolet rays from the sun have caused violent reactions.

We are living in a new era of petrochemical carcinogens. World War II marked a turning point in the growth of chemical industries. It is not certain that an informed populace will respond to the need for special-purpose legislation and regulatory controls. An outcry from the American public when matters are called to their attention would do much to help bring about these controls. A return to a simpler way of living would help. Sadly, however, greed and corruption rule over common sense, concern, compassion, and humanity's greater needs.

Generally, everything points to confusion and the need for corrective action on all fronts—in industry, in politics, and in the home. The barrage of media coverage of environmental and occupational cancer disasters has awakened a considerable segment of the population. Individually, we each need to be terribly aware and to make others aware as well.

What We Drink

Do you ever wonder why your tapwater tastes so bad? Perhaps yours doesn't; if so, your city may be one of the few places in this country where the level of chlorine used to purify the water supply is not as great. Chlorine is, after all, a poison gas. Yet no one questions the need for adding it to our drinking water to safeguard us against typhoid fever. It is a recognized fact that the addition of chlorine to water is the public-health measure that has just about wiped out typhoid.

Where does typhoid come from? Human excrement. Where does a town's raw, untreated sewage go? Into our lakes and rivers. So we all drink chlorinated water when we drink water that comes from the tap. Harald J. Taub, Executive Editor of *Prevention* magazine, in his eye-opening book *Keeping Healthy in a Polluted World,* says what we all think: treated water is no treat.

Taub reports that there has never been an organized, thorough investigation of the effect of chlorinated water on human—or even animal—health. He asks why, then answers by pointing to one competent physician (Dr. Joseph M. Price of Saginaw, Michigan) who has made his own extensive studies and concluded that chlorinated water causes heart disease. It is not a conclusion that has been generally accepted. But neither has it been investigated. In fact, it has been ignored.[3]

"What, after all, would happen if there were general agreement that the very same additive to drinking water that protects us from typhoid and other diseases—*and for which we have no substitute*—is at the same time a dangerous pollutant causing diseased arteries and heart attacks? Think of the turmoil. Think of the attacks on all the city governments and associations of water engineers and chemical manufacturers and users of chlorinated water in food processing. Think of the panic!

"No wonder nobody wants to stick his neck out, or even look into the question, for fear he might reach conclusions that would force him to stick his neck out. . . ."[4]

Taub points readers to Dr. Price's book entitled *Coronaries, Cholesterol, Chlorine.* Prior to 1900 heart disease was almost unheard of. In the last six to seven decades of human history, chlorination of water gained acceptance. Even Dr. Paul Dudley White, a name quickly recognized by most people as a leading cardiologist, has written that he did not see his first heart attack of the type caused by atherosclerosis until after 1920. Sir William Osler, another great physician whose name is associated with heart disease, lectured in 1910 and never mentioned this type of heart attack. Today it is the leading cause of death in the United States. "Clinical disease from atherosclerosis takes ten to twenty years to develop. The correlation between the introduction and widespread application of chlorination of water supplies and the origin and increasing incidence of heart attacks . . . is exceedingly difficult to explain away."[5]

Elsewhere I discuss in more detail cellular activity. Here it should be pointed out that DNA is nucleic acid, the material containing the programmed instructions for the cells of our bodies. Anything that injures DNA is potentially a health menace. Japanese scientists have discovered that chlorine chemically alters nucleic acids. What is supposed is that damaged nucleic acid is replaced with new, undamaged nucleic acid. But Japanese scientists tell us that chlorine also affects the precursors of nucleic acids. Can these damaged forerunners form into healthy nucleic acid? The amount of chlorine we get from water may be small, but our bodies are involved in a continual struggle to keep replacing damaged vital materials. The older we get, the more our bodily functions slow down. Combined with our threats to health and other invasions and attacks against our cellular system, we need to take all the precautionary measures we can.

Those measures will, for the most part, be things we can do for ourselves within our homes. We can boil our water for three minutes, as Taub recommends, thus removing 65 to 70 percent of the chlorine. This water, stored in glass containers with tops closed, can be used for drinking and cooking. Some families choose to install charcoal filters on their water taps; others buy bottled water.

The one thing that remains as a potential contaminant in water, regardless of whether boiled or filtered, is nitrate. Evidence is conclusive that nitrate is a potential cause of cancer. What is it? Nitrate is an essential plant food. Farmers spread chemical fertilizers with a high nitrate content over their farmland. Winter snows, spring thaws, and rain carry the runoff from farmlands into streams. It is not only chemical nitrates which cause trouble; animal and poultry wastes also contain generous amounts of nitrate. And then there is always human sewage. The greatest threat comes with the biochemical transformations that take place in and out of our bodies—bacterial action that changes nitrate into *nitrite*.

Have you ever heard of a baby found dead in its crib? It could be chemical suffocation. Babies have weak stomach acidity. Given a bottleful of water or formula sufficiently polluted with nitrate, the bacteria in the baby's stomach turns out nitrites so abundantly that, combined with red blood cells, they are rendered incapable of carrying oxygen.

What an adult might be able to tolerate because of sheer size, an infant cannot.

All of this is overwhelming to the untrained individual to comprehend. I can tell you that *nitrosamines* are known to cause cancer. What are they? Nitrites in the stomach combine with what is called *secondary amines* to form compounds known as *nitrosamines*. Do you know much more than when you started?

Next question: where do the secondary amines come from? Fish, cereal, tea, powdered milk, sausage, much cooked and processed foods, various grains, alcoholic beverages, and—even if *you* don't smoke, if you inhale someone else's smoke—secondary amines. Are you ready to throw up your hands and forget the whole thing? Are you thinking that if what we are saying is correct then everyone in the country should have cancer?

Wait a moment—this book is concerned with *prevention*. Why are some of us repeatedly telling the American public that they need to fortify their diets with vitamins and minerals? (I prefer to call them concentrated nutrients.) There are things we can all do, things we should be doing as precautionary measures for ourselves and our loved ones.

Am I telling you that nitrites can be wiped out in the stomach? Precisely. Brilliant biochemist Albert Szent-Gyorgyi and Nobel-prize-winning Dr. Linus Pauling have been credited with revolutionary discoveries with regard to vitamin C. An equally impressive list of scientists around the world have long advocated that this vitamin be routinely taken as a precautionary measure against a host of threats to our health.

Are you on prescription drugs? I hope you are taking adequate amounts of vitamin C. The question is rightly asked, "Why gamble with cancer when prevention is so simple and so inexpensive?"

Vitamin C, also known as ascorbic acid, not only has a stabilizing effect in one's system on nitrites, but it is capable of detoxifying hundreds of harmful chemicals that find their way into our bodies. Vitamin C—what a friend!

When you stop and think of the ever-present pesticides, detergents (detergent residue left on our dinnerware and in our clothing), chemical salts, fertilizers, dangerous chemicals, and even radioactive wastes—impurities in what we drink and breathe everyday—the recognition comes quickly that the human body requires all the help it can get to stay healthy.

What We Eat

"Your food shall be your medicine and your medicine shall be your food."

You might know that it was Hippocrates who made that statement. There are some of us who believe that 86 percent (or more) of all cancer conditions could be adequately treated and/or prevented by diet alone. I think Hippocrates would have agreed.

Why is it that so many people—well trained, intelligent people, as well as those with lesser intelligence—scoff at diet as a means of treating the cancer victim? Many of these people take better care of their pets and their registered cattle and horses than they do of themselves and their family members.

Dr. Dean Burk, formerly of the National Cancer Institute, compiled a list of known carcinogens including: 1) many food dyes, such as the triphenylmethane dyes and the napthylamine azo benzol dyes; 2) synthetic mucilage carboxymethyl cellulose, used as a stabilizer in processed cheese, French dressing, many dairy products, syrups, and artificially sweetened canned fruits; 3) residual arsenicals from pesticides and animal feed additives; 4) estrogenic chemicals used in fattening poultry and livestock (DES and other hormone-type chemicals): 5) food wrapping and coating materials composed of polymerized carbon and silicon compounds;6) insufficiently refined paraffins and mineral oils sometimes used to wrap cheese and fruits; 7) potential carcinogens from foodstuffs grown in polluted soil or water including arsenicals, selenium, and polycyclic hydrocarbon which may have been picked up, absorbed, and retained by the foods while in growing.

Dr. Harold W. Harper says the "wholesale tampering with natural nutrition has triggered the modern plagues of mankind, the degenerative killer diseases, which are the maladies caused not by bacteria, viruses and parasites, but by the continual ingestion of unnatural food."

There is mounting evidence that virtually every bite of food you eat has been treated with some chemical somewhere along the line: additives, coloring agents, bleaches, emulsifiers, preservatives, antioxidants, buffers, flavors and flavor enhancers, acidifiers, extenders, thickeners, artificial sweeteners—the list could go on and on. These things meant to enhance, enrich, color, preserve, and entice may be connected with the induction of cancer.

Consider this: since 1958 the Food and Drug Administration has approved the use of more than 3000 food additives as "Generally Recognized As Safe" (GRAS) and placed them on the official GRAS list. But the actual number of chemicals that go into denaturalizing our food is not known, and estimates vary widely. Some claim it is as high a 10,000. Over half of these additives are added simply to entice us to buy more foods so that the food-processing company will make a larger profit. Otherwise, the additives are entirely unnecessary. These chemicals and other ones used in the actual processing turn natural foods into adulterated simulations devoid of most of their nutrients, artificially colored and padded with preservatives, bleaches, texture enhancers, dough conditioners, and a large variety of other things.[6]

The average housewife who goes into the market to purchase her week's supply of groceries for her family is at the mercy of the FDA and those who control the GRAS List. The tragedy is that she is so uninformed. No mother would intentionally feed her family poisons over an extended period of time. How long those poisons stay in an individual's system, and what the danger is in terms of cumulative effect, is anybody's guess. Many items on the GRAS list have been submitted to only minimal testing—perhaps only short-term experiments or those involving small test-animal populations. (For example, if a carcinogen will cause cancer in 1 percent of the population, and 50 rats are fed the substance, in theory it will affect only one-half of one rat and might easily be overlooked in evaluating the experiment. That same substance would cause cancer in 1 percent of the human population—some 200,000 people.)

At least 7000 more additives in use are *not* on the GRAS list. George P. Larrick, former FDA Commissioner, admits that "our scientists do not know whether they [1/3 of additives] are safe or not, but they suspect some ought not to be in use." The Public Health Service says "it can be assumed ¼ of untested additives may be found capable of causing cancer." Virtually nothing is known of the results of mixing two or three additives in the body's system, even though each may be on the GRAS list.

Plainly, civilized man is polluting himself to death. As Dr. Harper points out, we run absolutely no risk of increased "population explosion" since, if degenerative disease continues to kill, maim, and cripple on the scale it has already reached, the Western world will lose a major portion of its population in a relatively short period of time.[7]

I have already introduced you to the subject of nitrites. Sodium nitrite is a food preservative much in use which kills botulism and keeps meat red. Some 8 billion pounds per year go into hot dogs, sausages, and canned hams. Since food processors are allowed to use only so much nitrite, they add *nitrate* to meat products and allow for chemical actions to turn it to *nitrite,* just to keep the meat red longer.

The word "nitrosamines" has been introduced. These nitrosamines cause cancer in virtually every type of tissue in virtually all animal tests. Over a thousand drugs contain secondary and tertiary amines, including the much-used Librium, Contac, Ritolin, Streptomycin, Allergen. A dose of only two ppm (parts per million) of nitrosamines (the lowest level tested) has induced cancer in rats, and there is a known cumulative effect. Cured pork and dried beef contain from 11 to 48 ppm; bacon left more than 100 ppm *after* cooking. Some nitrosamines have produced cancer after only one dose, while certain others may not affect an adult woman but increase the possibility of leukemia in her unborn child.

Dr. William Lijinsky of the Oak Ridge National Laboratory in Tennessee found nitrites in all kinds of cured and smoke-flavored meats. In Dr. Lijinsky's experiments, he fed nitrites in conjunction with secondary amines (present in wines, tea, fish, and in most drugs, including nonprescription analgesics, which so many Americans take) to laboratory rats. He found malignant tumors in 100 percent of the test animals. Says Dr. Lijinsky, "Nitrites constitute our worst cancer problem. I don't touch any of that stuff when I know nitrite has been added."

William Goodrich, former general counsel for the FDA, when asked by Congressman H.L. Fountain why the FDA didn't enforce a labeling regulation for nitrite in smoked fish, replied: "If you declare it on the label it simply precipitates the correspondence between us and the public asking why we allow this horrible thing in food. . . ."

Dr. Roger Williams, world-famous scientist and best-selling author, urges that nutritional illiteracy be abolished and that nutritional information be allowed to filter down. Mothers need to invest their time in becoming informed through reading books, magazine articles, and attending lectures on nutrition. The problem encountered is one of knowing who to believe, since there are books by cultists, self-appointed food specialists, and faddists. Some of the so-called health columns in newspapers and magazines are not written by prevention-oriented men and women. The information they provide is misleading and erroneous.

Educational information can be obtained from certain groups who are advocates of wholistic, metabolic, and preventive medicine. In addition to working to inform one's self, a search should be made to find a competent nutritionist. How do you determine whether such a person is prevention-oriented? Look for someone who has formal training in biochemistry as well as clinical experience with knowledgeable doctors.

Not to seek methods of change is to risk the continued impoverishment of natural processes.

Another offending area for the conscientious individual to eliminate is convenience foods. That may come as an upsetting blow to today's busy homemaker and the working woman. These foods may be convenient, but they are contrary to every rule of health imaginable. The profiteers in the food business have fed the consumer a line. Along with their beautifully packaged foods, they are serving us a heaping portion of poison. Read the labels. See what is added. Much of what you read you won't understand, and so you assume that if it's in food it must be safe. After all, the government wouldn't allow food manufacturers to market something that wasn't good for you.

The government is not God. Conflicts of interest exist. The government regulatory agencies work closely with big drug companies, the sugar industries, purveyors of drugs and medicines, and food processors. Dr. Michael Jacobson, codirector of a study group called the Center for Science in the Public Interest, has gone on record as accusing eminent American nutritionists of having "traded their independence for the food industry's favors." Dr. Jacobson states: "One can only come to the conclusion that industry grants, consulting fees, and directorships are muzzling, if not prostituting, nutrition and food-science professors."[8]

Snack foods, the breakfast-food section of the supermarket, baby foods, Jellos, white breads, processed cheeses (to name just a few of some of the more-commonly-used foods) are best left on the shelves of your favorite food market, as Jacqueline Verrett and Jean Carper state in the title of their best-selling book *Eating May Be Hazardous to Your Health.*

Of their findings, Ralph Nader said, "This is a soberly gripping book by a courageous Food and Drug Administration scientist and a lucid consumer writer. The story they tell about the silent violence in your food—how it got there and the FDA's abysmal lack of courage to make the food companies obey the law—makes you want to do something about it."

Of this information *Publisher's Weekly* stated: "The facts are startling, the conclusions frightening."

Beatrice Trim Hunter, in her *Fact Book on Food Additives and Your Health* points out that these food additives are also common ingredients in powders, solutions, and ointments used to treat athlete's foot. That's more than a little startling, isn't it!

Why are additives allowed? Why is this done? Because of their cosmetic value (to make the products more eye-appealing), and to enhance *shelf* life—not your life, but shelf life.

Ethel Renwick, in her book *Let's Try Real Food,* asks why, when we can serve delicious desserts made from fresh eggs, milk, cheese, fruit, pure gelatin, natural flavors, natural colors, and natural goodness, we should choose a convenience "foodless" frozen dessert that lists on its label these ingredients: water, sugar, hydrogenated vegetable oil, nonfat dry milk, modified tapico starch, emulsifers (polysorbate 60, sodium stearoy l-2-lactylate, sorbitan monostearate), vanilla extract, sodium casseinate, dextrose, salt, calcium carrageenan, guar gum, with artificial color and flavor.[9]

She points out that not all of those additives are dangerous, but some are complex chemicals, some are thought to need more researching, and some are known to be harmful. Is there honest food value in such a product? How many such products like this there are!

Blind experiments of massive proportions are being carried on under our very nose, or more appropriately, in our very mouths, for we are the human guinea pigs.

We fear, and rightly so, acute poisoning from foodstuffs—poisoning that would incapacitate or kill us within a short period of time. Food poisoning happens. But, as Verrett and Carper emphasize, "We now realize that far more critical than acute poisoning is the subtle, long-term, insidious poisoning of the body by certain chemicals that work slowly or cumulatively and whose ravages may not become evident for many years."[10]

The conscientious mother may think that she's sending her darling to school with a wholesome peanut-butter sandwich, but what she is probably doing is sending him to school with a sandwich filled with 22 percent hydrogenated oil, or "peanut-flavored cold cream."[11]

And additives are not the only offenders. Refined flour has been robbed of the very thing that God gave it with life-giving properties. The depleted white polished rice and the refined sugar are consumed by the average person to the tune of 104 to 170 pounds per year. There are actually people who are consuming more than their own body weight in sugar every year.

We are living in a world hostile to human health. There is no denying it. This chapter has barely skimmed the surface of the dangers to life and the prospects for longevity. The amazing thing is not that so many have already died from coronary disease and from cancer, but that so many manage to survive. Dr. Szent-Gyorgyi declares in *The Living State:*

> I am often shocked at the eating habits of people. What I find difficult to understand as a biologist is not why people become ill, but how they manage to stay alive at all. Our body must be a very wonderful instrument to withstand all our insults.

Radiation in Our Environment

In my book *Nutrigenetics* I point out that the term "empty calories" is often used. The reader needs to be alert to the fact that these are, in fact, sickness-breeding calories, or one might go so far as to call them malignant-contributing calories because they induce chronic, degenerative diseases due to their lack of nutrients which the body must have to utilize them. I call sugar Public Enemy Number 1, and white-flour products I refer to as Public Enemy Number 2. Not only do they have many things removed, but they have also suffered the addition of the antinutrition factors, the chemicals which are added to so many of our white-flour products in particular.

It would seem that one of the most insidious of all the contaminants which are cancer-producing is also the most neglected. Rarely does anyone hear about the fact that the man-made radiation in our environment today is becoming a major threat to our existence and a dominant part of the carcinogenic substances that are attacking the normal cell activities of our bodies.

The sight of 65,000 protestors in front of the U.S. Capitol on Sunday, May 6, 1979, with one purpose—opposition to nuclear power—brought President Carter out to respond. Chanting "No more nukes, No more Harrisburgs," the largest antinuclear-power crowd in U.S. history demonstrated peaceably. But they made their point.

It is a point more of us may need to echo in the years ahead if the government continues to think in terms of having 300 nuclear power plants in operation throughout the country by 1990. A plant disaster such as almost happened at Harrisburg would be devastating. Scientists connected with the government agency established to safeguard nuclear power plants (formerly the Atomic Energy Commission, recently renamed the Nuclear Regulatory Agency) admit that a significant leak of radioactivity from a nuclear plant would at the very minimum lead to 40,000 to 80,000 cancer deaths among those exposed individuals in the areas surrounding the plant.

One gram of gaseous radioactive plutonium released into

the atmosphere would be enough to eventually cause lung cancer in virtually every human being on earth. The land around a major nuclear-plant would be unusable for hundreds if not thousand of years. Any accident which would lead to an abnormal release of radioactivity (a break in the safety containers around a reactor or a broken pipe) would cause any or all of this.[12]

Many managers, scientists, and engineers have resigned their positions at nuclear power plants and with the Nuclear Regulatory Agency because of their concern. Not only is there concern about the safety and reliability of nuclear power, but the problem is monstrous about what to do with radioactive wastes. We are bequeathing a legacy of poison to our children and grandchildren.

Surgeon General Dr. Luther L. Terry (PHS) and Radiology Chief Donald R. Chadwick (AMA Journal, June 23, 1962) stated seventeen years before the 1979 demonstration: "There is no level of radiation exposure below which there can be absolute certainty that harmful effects will not occur to at least a few individuals when sufficiently large numbers of people are exposed."

The people in St. George, Utah, remember with bitterness the early 1950s, when the now-defunct Atomic Energy Commission (AEC) announced the times of experimental nuclear blasts, and the people climbed the bluffs at the end of town to watch the brilliant flashes. Mrs. Irma Thomas has been waging a one-woman war against government secrecy. "We were human guinea pigs," she states angrily. She has collected the names of nearly 200 people in St. George who have contracted cancer since 87 open-air nuclear blasts were set off by the AEC between 1951 and 1962. Thirty-nine on her list have already died.

The story is much the same in many of the communities in southwestern Utah, northern Arizona, and eastern Nevada, which were in the so-called "window" or prevailing wind direction that the AEC waited for time and again before setting off most of its nuclear devices. About 20,000 people lived in the "window" in the 1950s.

Opponents of atomic-bomb testing and atomic-power plants point out that radiation is the greatest contaminant in the world. No other contaminant compares with it. Radiation is tasteless, odorless, and colorless. It will be in your blood, in your bones, in your food, in the air, and will still be alive years later in your coffin (in your ashes).

Even Dr. Edward Teller, often called the father of the hydrogen bomb, has warned: "In principle, nuclear reactors are dangerous and do not belong on the surface of the earth."

The average American receives 100 millirems per year from cosmic rays, radioactive material in rocks, and other background sources. Another 100 millirems per person per year is activated through X-ray and other medical applications.

A Welsh physician, Dr. R.A. Holman, a bacteriologist, explains that life is essentially respiration, or oxidation. What has been happening to our respiratory systems is nothing short of alarming. Oxygen is essential for the removal and destruction of many toxic agents present on or in our cells. Dr. Holman maintains that "the more actively oxygenated our bodies are, the better we shall be able to combat the toxic agents which help to influence adversely our normal cells." The indiscriminate use of X-rays and the ever-present danger from radiation gives this doctor (and others of us) no small amount of concern.

Another physician, Dr. M. Burnet, writing in the South African *Practitioner* (no date) warns that radiation of all kinds —diagnostic X-ray, radioactive fallout, therapeutic X-rays, etc.—is extremely dangerous. Changes or mutations can be caused to happen in animals by experimental procedures with radiation. If in animals, why not in people?

Ralph Nader said before a senate hearing in 1968 that "The greatest source of man-made radiation . . . comes from medical and dental machines.'' Griffiths and Vallantine wrote in their book *Silent Slaughter,* "Twenty eight states . . . have absolutely no equipment requirements of any kind for mobile X-ray units, which X-ray tremendous numbers of people each year as they tour the country, and which are noted for their beat-up, overexposing equipment.''

Radiation is actually a term that is used for radiant energy, which is similar to radio and television waves. Radiant energy includes the waves that emanate from radioactive substances like radium or uranium, and of course from X-rays that are produced from the well-known X-ray machines. The radioactive substances give off several forms of rays; however, the ones that produce benefits are called gamma rays.

The X-ray machine gives off rays that are similar to the gamma rays but are more specifically known as Roentgen rays. These were named after Wilhelm Conrad Roentgen, who first discovered the presence of X-rays about 75 years ago. The Roentgen rays or gamma rays are the penetrating rays that come from the inside of the X-ray tube. These are the rays that are used in medical diagnosis and radiation therapy. They are also called ionizing rays and have the quality of penetrating an apparently solid object.

It does seem that wherever possible, we must minimize X-ray exposures. Dr. Ronald Glasser warns that "the overwhelming body of scientific evidence is that exposure to ionizing radiation, no matter how small, are at the very least additive, and that while we can't be sure at exactly what level of radiation exposure the DNA of a cell can be injured, the sensible course is to keep all exposures to the very minimum.''[13]

A paper published in the *World Health Organization Chronicle* entitled "Genetic Risks from Medical Radiation" puts the concern about radiation exposure in perspective:

> It has been known for a long time that irradiation of the skin may lead to cancer of the skin, irradiation of the bone marrow to leukemia, and irradiation of the thyroid to cancer of this

organ. Whole-body irradiation or irradiation of major parts of the body may shorten the life span, and irradiation of the gonads creates genetic changes, in particular an increased mutation frequency, which may result in hereditary diseases or in a deterioration of the level of health in future generations.[14]

Strange as it may seem, radiation is one of life's oldest enemies. I am referring to cosmic radiation. The only thing protecting mankind and all of life is the protective ozone encircling the globe. If the atoms of oxygen and ozone are reduced in depth, the poisoned rain of cosmic radiation will rain down upon us. The National Research Council has warned that a 10-percent decrease in the ozone of the atmosphere would permit enough excess ultraviolet radiation to reach the earth's surface to raise the incidence of skin cancer by 20 percent or more. With a further decrease in the ozone layer, more radiation would come through and, increased in intensity, would pass through our skin and hit the nuclei of the cells lying deeper in our bodies and finally, with an even greater increase in the bombardment, the genes in the nuclei of our sperm and eggs. Unheard and unfelt, the radiation will eventually cause all kinds of cancers and even (through mutation) the end of life itself.[15]

Genes, of course, are part of our chromosomes, which in turn are part of the cell's nucleus. It is the special chromosomes that are integrated into the reproductive systems of the parents that join in the creation of a child. The effect of radiation on the transmitters of our hereditary characteristics—our genes—is recognized as a grave potential danger. It should be pointed out that radioactive rays must reach the genital organs before any damage could occur. So it is always wise to shield and protect the reproductive glands so that these areas may not be damaged when diagnostic or therapeutic X-ray procedures are involved. It cannot be stressed sufficiently that proper personnel and procedures constitute a factor in the safe utilization of X-ray procedures.

The total radiation from the explosion of atomic and thermonuclear weapons has greatly increased our environmental radiation, and the thousands of tons of radioactive material that is ejected into the air will continue to give off radioactive activity for many years to come.

The process known as fission that gave mankind the ability to split the atom created a Pandora's box. The new elements that were created beyond the radioactive isotopes of other elements are now a part of our atmosphere on Planet Earth will be exerting deleterious effects on mankind for years to come.

Today we have many products that contribute to the total radiation of our environment—TV sets, microwave ovens and towers, the laser beam, food irradiation, and X-ray machines used to diagnose and treat malignancies and many other conditions, and used as tracers in the metabolic, circulatory, and hematologic conditions.

There has been a tendency to suppress information that might be related to the damages produced by man-made radioactive waves, and there certainly have been a limited number of protective messages given to the American people. In fact, the Atomic Energy Commission has always minimized the possibility of any ill effects from atomic-bomb testing, and has also emphasized that we do not have to worry about any atomic energy plants that are being built to help alleviate our energy crisis. There has also been a tendency by the manufacturers of equipment to subdue any apprehension about what is possible through the effects of waves from microwave ovens, microwave towers, and television sets.

The various X-ray machines that are used for security devices in airports, prisons, and in large office complexes are also additional sources of the ionizing rays.

The greatest threat to ourselves, to our children, and to our grandchildren's future is where it has always been—behind the clouds. That is not a farfetched statement. Why the controversy over supersonic aircraft? Why the concern over aerosol sprays? Large or small, each destroy ozone.

Now having pointed these things out to you, what can you do? I would emphasize that you obtain the books from which we have been quoting in this chapter.

Beyond that, here are some practical measures you can take:

1. Work at reducing your own personal contribution to pollution.

2. Do not be wasteful of materials and resources.

3. Conserve energy, electric power in particular. Think of the many appliances in your home you could do without or could use less often. Sixty million households joining in this effort would greatly minimize the load and would greatly improve the quality of modern living.

4. Use less paper (paper comes from wood—the trees that are cut down). Trees remove carbon dioxide from the air and convert it into oxygen.

5. Walk instead of drive whenever you can. Use a cheaper and smaller car that consumes less gasoline and runs on cheaper fuel.

6. Cut down on water use. Boil your tapwater for drinking and cooking purposes, or install a filter, or use bottled water.

7. Avoid processed foods; eat only lean meats and then no more than two or three times a week. Eat more seafood and poultry. Eat more uncooked fruits and vegetables, nuts and seeds.

We can do something about what we eat and drink. We can build up the cells of our respiratory system to aid us in fighting disease because of the air we breathe. But the thing that has been the most difficult for us to cope with has been the problem of man-made radiation. How can we protect ourselves against that? I think SOD is the answer.

Frank DeLuca's experimental work on superoxide dismutase, first in liquid form (to be diluted with distilled water and dropped under the tongue, as used by my daughter Phyllis) and then later the development of the product into a tablet, is a medical breakthrough as far as I am concerned. (See chapter 10, where we discuss the Cell-Assurance Program.)

If I am going to have X-rays, whether for my teeth, gallbladder, or whatever, I take SOD. If I walk in front of a microtower, I am being zapped. Most microwave ovens are well-protected, but it is the accumulative effect of radiation that concerns me. When I walk by an electrical motor I am getting some X-ray. It is all around us. We cannot avoid it. For this reason, SOD is a part of the preventive program my daughter now uses to prevent future cancerous tumors; it is a part of my own preventive program, and one that I advocate for my patients.

FOOTNOTES

1. Dr. Ronald J. Glasser, *The Greatest Battle* (New York: Random House, 1976), Preface.
2. Ibid.
3. Harald J. Taub, *Keeping Healthy in a Polluted World* (New York: Harper & Row, 1974), p. 75.
4. Ibid.
5. Ibid., p. 77.
6. Harold W. Harper, M.D., and Michael L. Culbert, *How You Can Beat the Killer Diseases* (New Rochelle, N.Y.: Arlington House, 1977), p. 34.
7. Ibid., pp. 55, 56.
8. Ibid., p. 40.
9. Ethel H. Renwick, *Let's Try Real Food* (Grand Rapids: 1976), p. 55.
10. Jacqueline Verrett and Jean Carper, *Eating May Be Hazardous to Your Health* (Garden City, N.Y.: 1974), p. 31.
11. Renwick, p. 164.
12. Glasser, p. 168.
13. Ibid., p. 165.
14. Ibid., p. 164.
15. Ibid., p. 151.

4

Very few people know what
real health is because most
are occupied with killing
themselves slowly.
—Albert Szent-Gyorgyi,
Nobel Prize Laureate

Cancer Charade

Our cancer research is misdirected, inefficient, and inadequate. We have almost as many people living off the disease as are dying from it. The government spends billions on cancer research, but at the same time allows known carcinogens in our processed foods, subsidizes cigarettes, and continues to develop new radiation, surgical, and chemotherapy techniques when burning, cutting, and poisoning have already proved largely unsuccessful. Physicians have not been trained in preventive medicine and, not having experience or knowledge of preventive medicine, they continue the outmoded but orthodox approach of treating symptoms rather than the entire body.

I know these are serious charges to be making, but the seriousness of the cancer epidemic demands that voices be raised to call attention to the cancer charade.

The confusion that exists in the minds of many is cause for concern. Misconceptions abound. Misinformation has been fed to us through the media. Newspapers, magazine articles, and books come at us with varying opinions that clash. Who and what is the public to believe? Those who hover on the brink of deciding in favor of developing a positive program of health for themselves and loved ones find themselves falling back into bad habits, developing physical problems, running to the doctor, and running the old treadmill of indecision. We are creatures bound by habits. Habits are hard to break. It is a vicious circle. In the meantime, valuable time is lost while our health as a nation declines.

The game of charades may be fun, but in real life, when one's health is at stake, or the health of a loved one, cancer is not fun and games. For years, I and other greatly concerned doctors who believe in preventive measures have sought to receive grants from the government to start a school for preventive medicine. At one time I took 15 proposals to Peter Borne, a psychiatrist on the White House staff, all to no avail. We are confronted with a fundamental problem of gigantic proportions: attitudes. When we should all be working together to fight the battle against disease, we find various groups within the medical profession and the government at variance with each other and with those of us in the forefront of what Dr. Roger J. Williams calls nutrition against disease.

Physicians are so busy trying to diagnose disease and prescribing prescriptions that they have little time to help patients think in terms of maintaining good health. The physician's role has changed drastically from what it was once thought to be. The charge has been leveled, and I agree 100 percent, that medical training today does not prepare the physician to recognize either the leading cause of noninfective disease or the related conditions for effective resistance of infections.

In simple terms, for the layperson, this means that what happens to our body cells is crucial to our health. We are talking about cellular malnutrition and deficiencies in our environment. What we eat, what we breathe, what we take into these bodies through our mouths and through our nostrils is contributing either to health and total physical and mental well-being, or else it becomes a precursor of ill health, disease, and a deterioration of the body forces that should and could be used to fight off and resist invading forces that attack our cells. Does this sound like warfare? It definitely is.

The medical profession is more concerned about curing disease than preventing or attacking the basic causes of disease. Lest this sound like I am coming down too hard on members of the profession, let me hasten to say that I am one of their number and understand their busyness. I also understand what has gone into their training—the precepts and procedures they have been taught. But the awareness needs to come that the ideology so consistently thrust upon medical students is not preparing them to help the individual prevent disease in the first place.

Dr. Roger Williams calls it a "breakdown-patchup" philosophy. It has to do with the physician's need to stay in business. Healthy people do not require the services of their doctor. In order to flourish, a business needs customers. Doctors are no different from other businessmen in this respect. It comes back to the fundamental problem of attitudes.

But doctors are not the only ones affected by this problem. Now we are getting to the nitty gritty, and it's called economics. Prevention-oriented approaches to helping sick people get well and helping well people stay healthy could spell ruin for the pharmaceutical industry as well as the loss of jobs for many related organizations. The problem is immense. It is so broad in scope that when you start to think about it your mind is boggled.

Endowments, donations, and gifts are being poured into university research and other research efforts to find a cure for cancer. Hundreds of thousands of people are on payrolls that would be affected if the health of this country were to improve for the better. Whether we want to admit it or not, disease is one of the biggest money-makers in our economy.

Vast sums are given to such organizations as the American Cancer Society (ACS), the American Medical Association (AMA), the National Cancer Institute (NCI), and other similar groups who are supposed to be in the vanguard of the struggle for combating disease. There are those of us, and the number is growing significantly, who wish that the public would channel some of those funds into the kind of research we are advocating—research aimed at prevention rather than at a fruitless search for miracle cures that do not exist. Who can dispute Nobel laureate Albert Szent-Gyorgyi and his observation that "Very few people know what real health is because most are occupied with killing themselves slowly."

Such self-destruction comes as we continue to undermine our health through faulty living habits. So long as the American public listens to the attacks being made upon those who are calling for research into the food industry, and seeking for environmental reforms, they are signing their own premature death warrants. Such irresponsible attacks are coming from many quarters—segments of medicine, industry, and government bureaucracy. Where are the men and women of conscience who will rise against the tide of those whose motives are subject to question, and others who (if not from the motive of profit) are at best uninformed and unwilling to open up their minds to the possibility that preventive medicine advocates may indeed be saying things they need to consider?

In biblical days if something was found within the camp that was not in the best interest of the people, and it was proven that this was so, the laws stated that such a one should be taken outside the camp and stoned to death. It was a bloody business. Today we do not stone those who deal treacherously against others, but we have departed far from guidelines which were meant to protect us from those whose intentions are subject to question.

Why is there such resistance among the medical profession, the government, and much of the public to an examination of ways of living and eating that can only bring radiant health, emotional stability, vigorous vitality, maximum endurance, and a consequent reduction in disease and ill health? It's a fair question, and one deserving of a reply by the opponents of preventive medicine.

Overlap and inconsistency between authorities of various regulatory agencies exist. Research programs have been poorly conceived. This is not to say that all research has been ineffective; significant strides have been made and much has been learned and gained, but inner conflict and struggle has crippled and greatly hampered the efforts of those whose heart is in their work. This abuse of power has stultified competitive scientific research. Pressure groups and lobbying forces have subverted the implementation of priorities for the prevention of cancer. These unresolved dilemmas create formidable tasks for those charged with the responsibility of moving research programs along. These are things which the average layperson is unaware of, but meanwhile tremendous sums continue to flow into the coffers of the leading agencies for cancer research. This represents an investment of dollars from the hard-working, well-meaning average American. What has been the returns for all the billions of dollars donated?

Dr. Samuel S. Epstein, Professor of Occupational and Environmental Medicine at the School of Public Health of the University of Illinois at the Medical Center in Chicago (and a prolific author of hundreds of scientific publications and books) treats the politics of cancer in a thoroughly documented book by that title calling attention to the indisputable fact that "In the last four decades there has been little overall improvement in our ability to treat and cure most cancers . . ." and "Over the last two decades, there has been no further significant improvement in overall cancer survival rates, nor in survival rates for major cancer sites such as lung, stomach, pancreas, and brain, which are still virtual death sentences, nor for breast, colon-rectum, prostate, cervic, and uterus, whose five-year survival rates continue to range from 45 percent to 75 percent, with little or no change as yet. These facts in no way diminish the importance of recent striking improvements in treatment and survival of some relatively rare cancers, especially Hodgkin's disease, Wilm's tumor, choriocarcinoma, and some leukemias."[1]

Generally, if you're one of the unfortunate victims who has a suspicious lump or bump and are told you have cancer by the doctor, the nurse will tactfully move the conversation around to questions about your insurance plan. She may even inquire about whether you have a will. They know and you know that a diagnosis of cancer is the pronouncement of possible earlier death than one had hoped for. It is a cutting short of one's plans for the future; a confrontation with reality; a step into the fear and unknowns that surround the cancer victim and his family. It is all this and much more. Too few will be among the patients who have remissions.

Despite public outcry for a cure, and billions of research dollars being spent, as Dr. Epstein and others of us are stating, the recovery rate from cancer is not encouraging. An international cancer conference estimated that 82 percent of those diagnosed will die within six months to five years; 16 percent will die after five years; 2 percent are considered healed by surgery.[2] Congressman J.W. Wydler questioned the National Cancer Institute's management of the war on cancer, noting that the number of cancer deaths has risen disproportionately in the period of greatest government spending on the cancer program. (Cancer deaths were up 4.2 percent in the period 1972-1975, following the combined public-private initiative War on Cancer launched when the National Cancer Act of 1971 provided funding for the National Cancer Institute.)

There are no satisfactory answers. At best they are weak excuses.

Cancer-phobia of families and victims and its death-image anxiety is accentuated by the mystique utilized by the charitable organizations that feed and flourish on this unfortunate factor. Fund-raisers talk about speeding up the research aimed at finding the cause and the cure of cancer. They persistently advance the idea that there will be a specific virus or similar causative agent for which a magic bullet, as it were, can be developed—a major cure for cancer.

Much of the public has read the misleading statements coming out of some of our leading cancer centers predicting such things as a cure for 85 percent of all cancer (within 10 years) by the multiple attack methods of surgery, chemotherapy, and radiation. One has to ask, "Does the track record indicate this sort of breakthrough?"

The American Cancer Society, headquartered in New York, where it was first incorporated as a non-profit organization around the time of the First World War, is seemingly the best organized of the disease-related charities. It has 58 chartered divisions with around 2800 local units. It has nearly 3000 paid staff members and oversees some 2½ million volunteers.

Most American science writers, the news media, and our elected representatives feel it politically expedient to beat the drums for the dictum that the best cancer cure is available only in the U.S.A. They point out that it must be the best because the NCI and the ACI are spending about a billion dollars a year to study it. They do not point out how much of this is being misspent and misdirected. Dr. Irwin Bross, Director of Biostatistics at the Roswell Park Memorial Institute of Cancer Research in Buffalo, New York, told legislators that the NCI's attempts at a cancer vaccine are "a fiasco—a waste of time, effort, and hundreds of millions of taxpayers' dollars."[3]

It appears, however, that results in most tumor cases are consistently better in Germany than here in the U.S. In Germany a number of therapies are used which are either outlawed here or are submerged in a mirage of "put-downs," which is a favorite technique of the Food and Drug Administration (FDA) and the NCI.

The controversy over Laetrile is a prime example of the reluctance and even unwillingness of the government to have an open mind about metabolic programs which such countries as Mexico have used with astonishing success in treating cancer victims. For people in this country to have to obtain court orders granting permission to receive and transport Laetrile from Mexico for cancer treatment is unthinkable; yet case after case exists where this has been necessary. (For more documentation on this, the reader is referred to the book *Cancer, Metabolic Therapy, and Laetrile.*)[4] One of the most widely publicized incidents involving FDA interference in the dispersal of Laetrile to terminally ill cancer patients took place in Tennessee. Gatlinburg businessman Doug Heinsohn went to battle with the FDA—a lengthy, costly, and involved wrangle with bureaucracy that touched off a nationwide revival of the debate over Laetrile. In the end, after edicts, red tape, regulations, and many delaying tactics, Heinsohn won.

It has become increasingly apparent that Laetrile is not the major arm in the treatment of cancer. It has, however, been a good rallying point for those persons who are becoming more aware that the individual must have freedom to choose the therapy that involves his own future health or that of members of his family.

Dr. Harold W. Manner in his marvelous book *The Death of Cancer* tells the story of research involving Laetrile that literally dropped a bombshell on orthodoxy. Dr. Manner is the much-esteemed Chairman of the Biology Department of Loyola University of Chicago. The research findings of Dr. Manner and graduate students has shown that Laetrile therapy is unorthodox but works. There are still many unanswered questions, and Dr. Manner and his students are dedicated to the proposition that disease can be prevented. Each dollar contributed to Loyola's Biology Department goes into his research efforts. There has been much antagonism to his work from some of the major bureaucracies of the country. Much more research is still needed.

The Institute of Cancer Research of Vienna University in Austria, as well as researchers in countries such as Finland, Sweden, Iceland, and other European countries, have demonstrated remarkable results in vitamin and enzyme therapy (more on this in succeeding chapters). Suffice it to say that scientists and doctors in the United States do not have a monopoly on intelligence, and that the American people stand to be the losers when they fail to keep an open mind about what others are doing and saying.

Anyone who has taken even a cursory look at the activities of the FDA can cite instances of inconsistency, irresponsibility, and blatant disregard for the public welfare. In many ways the FDA does little more than act as a rubber stamp for activities proposed by major food processors.

For that matter, the power that rests in the bureaucratic and political center of the U.S. in general is inconsistent in its approach to cancer when it allows the tobacco industry to continue producing cigarettes (with only a weak slap on the wrist, as it were, and a warning on the cigarette package that smoking is harmful to one's health). The same could be said of the sugar industry and the consumption of this extremely harmful food (if it can be called food). In his book *Sweet and Dangerous*, Dr. John Yudkin, a physician and biochemist who is currently Professor of Nutrition Emeritus at London University in England, amassed a formidable amount of information that demonstrated his premise that sugar is probably the leading cause of such disorders as hardening of the arteries, heart attacks, diabetes, gout, indigestion, ulcers, poor eyesight, unhealthy skin, and tooth decay. Why does the Sugar Association, a billion-dollar industry, lobby in Washington to influence government decisions?

And isn't it interesting that few hospitals ban cigarette smoking in their rooms or have discontinued cigarette-vending machines? (Even the American Cancer Society admits that cigarette smoking is the cause of at least 80 percent of all lung cancers.)

It is hoped that publicity on alternate nontoxic therapy for cancer will spotlight the cold fact that a patient does not have complete freedom of choice of therapy for his condition. Opponents of nontoxic therapies claim that patients are spending several thousand dollars for this treatment. True—and it is a pitiful pittance compared to the large amount spent for surgery, chemotherapy, radiation, hospitals, and attending physicians—a failure in cancer therapy. (It is not uncommon for "terminal" cancer patients' families to spend $50,000 before the victim succumbs.)

The cancer victim and his family are in actuality left to the mercy of the attending physician. One can only hope and pray that more and more doctors will come to see the wisdom in looking beyond surgery, chemotherapy, and radiation to the wisdom of the ages and nutritional approaches to reverse the cellular disturbance which has invaded the body of the cancer patient. Over and over again I shall repeat in this book in one way or another that cancer arises from poisoning of the cells. As the body wages war against the poisoning, it uses up its strength in a vain attempt to regenerate the damaged cells. Swedish biochemist Dr. Henning Karstroem maintains that "impaired cellular respiration causes cancer." The idea is that healthy development of cells is prohibited, and instead they are driven to unhealthy growth and abnormal multiplication. The tumor is the end result of this battle. The lumps and bumps are often the first indication that something has gone awry.

Ideally, the attending physician will have an open enough mind to listen to the cancer victim who may have a smattering of information and plead for nutritional therapy. As in the case of my daugher Phyllis, you will note that I did not suggest to her husband that he reject the advice of their internist friend. Patient and physician should have the freedom to choose what is needed to sustain the victim in all aspects of his dilemma.

The doctor's motive should be what is in the best interests of the patient. It is difficult to conceive that any doctor should be more interested in the monetary profit which may accrue to him for his needed services than the ultimate well-being of the patient. Whether a doctor will include other forms of therapy for his patients besides the usual methods approved by the medical hierarchy will depend on the patient's knowledge of things discussed in this and similar books, and his ability to convince his doctor that he wishes a wise combination of therapies to be employed.

Not every cancer victim has a father who is a doctor interested in bringing about a metabolic balance with protective (cell-wise) dieting that is balanced in needed nutrients. With the cooperation of my daughter, her husband, and her internist, we were able to start Phyllis on a program that arrested her cancer, enabled her to put on weight, and feel like a new woman.

Too many individuals, however, abdicate responsibility for their health to what Ivan Illich in the book *Medical Nemesis* labels what appears to be "an omnipotent health care system." Illich maintains that the average person has developed an "inordinate confidence in medical miracles," and consequently does little or nothing to try to improve his own health. The thinking seems to be that the all-powerful medical establishment is on call 24 hours a day, and if illness strikes, the doctors, nurses, and technicians will be there to pick up the pieces (for a price, of course). But then, there's always one's insurance to fall back on. What such individuals fail to consider is that a physician may succeed in putting the pieces back together, or in taking something (a cancerous tumor, for instance) out, but rarely is that same physician able to restore what someone has called "a high level of wellness."

We pay for our indulgences and foolishness in expensive ways—our health! And in the end, we pay with our very lives.

Oncology is the study and treatment of tumors. It was first recognized in the United States in 1973 as a medical speciality. An oncologist is a doctor who specializes in the study of cancer in one form or another. An oncologist friend of mine was trained under the benevolent scrutiny of Big Brother for his oncology training. He is very compassionate, but he will not touch any drug or try any new technique that has not wormed its way through the so-called credibility of voluminous infor-pile at the NCI, the FDA, and his oncology training center. He well knows that if he tries anything outside the protocol he will risk the wrath of his colleagues and lose his status as the oncologist in his specialized field.

There are those of us who are calling for a demystifying of cancer. Misconceptions need to be cleared up both for the benefit of the public and for those within the ranks of the medical profession. We have had enough of the cancer charade. But rigidity, apathy, ignorance of alternative therapy, busyness that precludes the possibility of keeping up with the normal diffusion of knowledge in medical circles, resistance to innovations in treatments (whether conscious or not), and always the threat of malpractice suits prevents most doctors from looking beyond or even being willing to experiment outside accepted orthodox methods. For some, the knowledge that cancer prevention could put them out of work, or greatly cut down on their practice, seems to only enforce their reluctance. Unfortunately, many doctors today are committed in their mind to the straitjacket placed on them by their medical training. They consider mainly the drugs being touted in their medical journals and at the medical meetings that are a part of the medical hierarchy. Some of them learn mainly from the drug salesmen who call on them with such efficient regularity, generously doling out samples.

One has to wonder about the medical profession's sense of values when nurses throughout Texas (the state in which I live) are invited to attend a three-week training session plus an annual refresher seminar to provide them with new diagnostic techniques, current education referral, and follow-up techniques, but there is so little attention paid to a meaningful cancer prevention program—a program that would include thorough, valid nutritional data which would enable them to inform patients. Often it is the nurse who sees the patient and ends up having more time with the cancer victim than the attending physician. What a world of good the nurses could accomplish if they were better informed about the nutritional way to combat disease, about the metabolic processes, and about the need for therapeutic augmentation of concentrated nutrients (vitamins and minerals)!

The cancer charade is a snarl of confusion for the average person who relies so heavily upon his doctor and the usual orthodox treatment with its generally unfavorable survival rate and the poor prognosis that usually accompanies chemotherapy and the radiation therapy.

Patients are influenced by the hopelessness and fear that grips the hearts and minds of their loved ones. This can produce a mental block that does not allow them to think in terms of the total approach to the prevention of cancer.

It is lamentable that many people do not understand that physicians can only prescribe for the alleviation of symptoms. The real power of the body is its enormous capacity to ward off disease, including cancer. Your body doesn't want cancer! People have not thought sufficiently of the protective power of the body to go to work to protect itself against the hostility of our environment—that which we eat and breathe. We must learn that prevention does not come in a prescription of alleviating drugs. No doctor or druggist can do for you what you can far better do for yourself—take care of yourself. There is more power in a prayer than in a prescription.

The great tragedy and travesty of American medicine is exemplified in the lack of interest in what the patient eats and drinks, and then what happens to what we put in our mouths. The travesty that orthodox medicine prescribes antacids for poor digestion is appalling. The fact that orthodox medicine confuses obesity and "overnutrition" is astonishing. Given our modern processed convenience foods, it is virtually impossible to be overnourished; obesity is a sure sign of malnutrition of a definite sort.

The largest stumbling block to putting in proper perspective and then understanding and treating cancer has been the medical establishment's inability to utilize available nutritional knowledge. With such an understanding passed on to one's patients, the average doctor would quickly see a great reduction in the number of cancer victims. Prevention is, always has been, and always will be the name of the game.

Nutritional balance has become more understandable as the curtains of mystery that surround cell function are parted. How much I regret that the public is not aware of this reluctance among the medical profession to accept this well-established and reasonable approach to the prevention of the chronic degenerative diseases, including cancer.

Certainly it is apparent there is too little research directed toward optimum nutrition, detoxification, immunology, the psychological processes, mental and spiritual well-being, and the nontoxic metabolic therapies, all of which offer hope in the alleviation of the pain and suffering of cancer victims.

It seems incongruous that of the $800-million-plus annual budget of the NCI, only $6 million is spent on nutritional research—especially when mounting research from private labs and sources suggests that cancer is the final stage of a long pathological degeneration largely due to nutritional deficiencies, antinutrition, and subsequent metabolic imbalance.

Dr. Irwin Bross (mentioned earlier in this chapter) alleges that federal cancer research goes to "laboratory scientists who have no real interest in . . . human cancer and who couldn't care less about prevention of human diseases." He maintains that if even half of these vaccine researchers' time were put into an effective primary prevention program, we would be well on our way to the actual conquest of cancer. Dr. Bross states that a lot of the money that congress voted for the cancer program has been "wasted on scientific boondoggles such as the worthless cancer vaccine program."[5] He further stated that many programs are "little more than public relations gimmicks . . . paper tigers to reassure the concerned American public that something is being done when it isn't."[6]

Hardly anyone would argue that cancer and the other disease killers shouldn't be stopped, but the plethora of diverse partial solutions we hear is not the answer. Waiting for the telltale danger signs of cancer is not the solution. Detecting cancer early is, or course, a valid medical advance, but waiting until tissue changes make their ominous show is usually too late. Early detection helps, but it is not the answer either.

What then is the answer?

It is late. We must awaken to the fact that we need a total biocellular approach with the necessary spiritual and psychological measures to sustain maximum health. We must not be fooled by the tendency of many scientific researchers to look at one part of the body and think they will find the answer to cancer in that one area. Cancer is not a local disease; the malignancy epidemic cannot be solved by the microscopic study of the structures of abnormal tissues. Cancer is a disease that affects the entire body, and therefore it must be considered a problem of the total body, mind, and spirit. Our present treatment and research plans are not solving the problem. We must remember *God's answer—prevent it!*

> Do you not know that you are a temple of God, and that the Spirit of God dwells in you? If any man destroys the temple of God, God will destroy him, for the temple of God is holy, and that is what you are.
>
> —1 Corinthians 3:16, 17 NASB

In Old Testament times we see the people being reprimanded for their neglect of the temple of worship. Abuse and misuse created problems that had to be dealt with severely. Plainly, God intended that the place where people worshiped Him be treated with respect.

Just so our bodies, as human temples, are to be treated with respect. To defile them is to risk incurring the displeasure of a holy God who has plainly stated through the Apostle Paul that we are to give them proper care.

FOOTNOTES

1. Samuel S. Epstein, M.D., *The Politics of Cancer* (San Francisco: Sierra Club Books, 1978), p. 329.
2. Ebba Waerland, *Cancer, A Disease of Civilization* (St. Catharines, Ontario: Provoker Press, 1970), p. 2.
3. Harold W. Harper, M.D., and Michael L. Culbert, *How You Can Beat the Killer Diseases* (New Rochelle, N.Y.: Arlington House, 1977), p. 118.
4. Douglas L. Heinsohn, *Cancer, Metabolic Therapy, and Laetrile* (Sevierville, Tenn.: 1977).
5. Harper and Culbert, pp. 117-118.
6. Ibid., p. 118.

5

It is not God's will that we must have so many sudden deaths, heart attacks, and strokes. It is certainly our fault. We must accept the challenge, and having done so, do so much more about it than we have in the past.
—Paul Dudley White, eminent cardiologist

Cancer's Companions

Self-help health. Is that terminology new to you? Do-it-yourself kits, books, and projects abound. So why not self-help health? Not too surprisingly, that's what is happening across the country. It may be a result of disillusionment with established health-care facilities, crowded conditions, long waits in doctor's offices, and the spiraling medical costs. Or it may have something to do with the proliferation of books on the subject of nutrition and health, and the magazine articles and columns dealing with the subject. Whatever the reason, people are searching for answers to their health problems and making serious attempts to rid themselves of ill health and disease. We applaud such efforts when common-sense is applied and an intelligent approach is used. Certainly self-help health is one sure way to reduce medical costs. We need to learn how to stay healthy; and we must discipline ourselves to stay away from those things that we know are detrimental to health.

If you want to avoid $150- to $300-a-day hospital-room costs, skyrocketing medical-insurance costs, enormous medical fees and salaries, drugs pushed by the pharmaceutical cartel, and an ever-expanding armamentarium of expensive gadgetry of all kinds designed to provide the latest diagnostic techniques for a civilization that is getting sicker and sicker, then you will study with earnestness the facts presented in this book and others of a related nature.[1]

An Introduction to Nutrigenetics

During my early practice days in Kansas City, I was called to a rooming house and attended a male patient, 43 years of age, who succumbed to a heart attack within a short time after I arrived at his room. This distressed me. I thought, "Why doesn't every 43-year-old man die of a heart attack? Why this man?"

Shortly after that, I was assisting on an operation on a 24-year-old female whose gallbladder was full of stones and had to be removed. This also piqued my intellectual curiosity, and I thought a great deal about why this particular 24-year-old woman should have to have her gallbladder removed, and why not every other 24-year-old woman.

These reflections led me to the conclusion that there are genetic factors which tend to program individuals for the development of certain diseases, and it also pointed out that there had to be other factors. I concluded that the weakest link in our health chain was nutrition. This led me to the coining of the word *nutrigenetics*—the inference that poor genes plus poor food leads to poor health.

My inclination to include nutrients in the alleviation of symptoms and the prolongation of optimum health, and the prevention of the chronic degenerative diseases, led me to use massive doses of Vitamin C intravenously in the early 1940s. Since I had taught in medical school, I felt it imperative to impart this information to many of my former and present students. So the therapeutic effectiveness of this particular therapeutic technique was well-proven in the minds of many of my colleagues. This has now become a very useful tool in the therapeutic treatment of many forward-thinking physicians.

Only You Can Come to the Rescue of Your Cells

Much of what happens to us physically is not our own fault. Many individuals have inherited poor genetic patterns, and it is the genes in our cells that give us the blueprint for our potential metabolism. Most of the action that takes place in the cell that we are concerned about is in the little furnace, called the mitochondria, and that is where the energy exchange takes place. This is where poor-genetic-pattern problems occur. We see it particularly in obese people.

This means that if you have a faulty genetic pattern and eat poor foods—foods that do not supply the right nutrients in the right amounts in the right form—you are going to have poor health. You will have cholesterol problems, or blood-sugar problems, or triglycerides (another blood fat), or those ugly fat deposits under the skin. Any or all of these and other degenerative diseases—diseases of the whole body and of metabolic processes that make up what I call the *metabolic dysequilibrium syndrome*—make you a potential risk for a shorter life span, or a life characterized by ill health and all the pain, discomforts, and limitations that go along with diseased bodies.

But even though you may have inherited poor genetic patterns, there is still something you can do, and in fact *must* do, to help yourself, to correct deficiencies, to come to the rescue of your cells, and to improve your chances for optimum health.

The Metabolic Disequilibrium Syndrome

That is a mouthful—*metabolic disequilibrium syndrome —but it is really very important for you to understand that you have two kinds of metabolism in your body. You have anabolic* metabolism, which is the build-up phase. Children are in the anabolic phase because they are constantly growing; as we get older, we are supposed to be in metabolic balance, not breaking down any more than we are building up daily. Most of us, unfortunately, are in the *catabolic* state. Catabolic metabolism is the break-down state, and that is actually where we get the term "break-down diseases" or chronic, degenerative diseases.

It is vitally important that you rebuild and repair what you destroy every day so that you stay in metabolic balance. Many elderly people, especially those you see in old people's homes or care centers, are in the catabolic stage. This is one of the great tragedies hovering over the American scene.

Keeping Yourself Together

A house will be no stronger than the materials used in the building process. That is an apt illustration of the human body. Collagen is the gluelike substance that holds your cells together, comparable to the mortar and cement in a building. Understandably, when your collagen is strong, you can anticipate fewer physical problems associated with aging. Similarly, when it is defective, your body begins to break down. This doesn't happen all at once; over the years, cell walls lose their firmness, and the defective collagen goes to pieces, gets weak and weepy, and leaks uselessly into the bloodstream. The result is arthritis, muscle aches, or serious destruction of bone or blood vessels. Other signs of collagen deficiency are low-back pain, gout, and general inflammation of muscle tissues, causing aches and pains. The stigma of aging is associated with wrinkles, loss of teeth, and other effects that we'd rather not talk about.

You Can Make Old Age Wait

What can be done? How do we make old age wait? How can we be sure of a good collagen supply?

Optimal amounts of vitamin C and the bioflavanoids are one of the first lines of defense. These are easy to obtain (and are enjoyable from citrus fruits, for example). The membrane on the fruit is a source of those valuable bioflavanoids. But you will still need the help of the therapeutic augmentation of concentrated nutrients.

The cumulative effect of DDT, lead, food additives, and other toxic substances which we have taken into our system for years slows down hormone and enzyme activity. Vitamin C is used in the detoxification process by the liver. But this valuable vitamin is quickly used up with each job it performs. As you grow older, it is called upon to perform more and more.

Stress also uses up vast quantities of the vitamin C in one's body. And people who smoke or use drugs need to be particularly aware of what is happening to their system and to the vitamin C they take in.

It was Adelle Davis years ago who first alerted many people to what was happening to their foodstuffs and how the proper selection of foods and supplements could hasten recovery from illness. She pointed out in her widely read book *Let's Get Well* that all diseases are caused by chemicals, and all diseases can be cured by chemicals.

What Kind of Chemicals?

"All the chemicals used by the body—except for the oxygen which we breathe and the water which we drink—are taken in through food. If we only knew enough, all diseases could be prevented, and could be cured, through proper nutrition," Mrs. Davis was fond of stating.

Old age is simply the result of tissues becoming damaged and lacking what is called "tissue integrity." This means they lack the chemicals of good nutrition. You can make old age wait by making sure you provide your tissues with that which will enable them to repair themselves. Correct the nutritional deficiencies that exist in your body, and you will see a difference in your appearance. What's more, you will feel more agile and your entire body will respond in more youthful ways. The aging process can be slowed down and even reversed. What woman doesn't want to be charming and vivacious after she has reached the half-century mark and well beyond? And what man doesn't want to maintain his virility and vitality throughout his life span?

The writer of Proverbs pointed out that "A wise man is strong, and a man of knowledge increases power" (Proverbs 24:5 NASB). Our total well-being is at stake; the reason we are *not* so strong is that our eating habits have fallen so far amiss from what the Creator intended them to be. We are to be guardians of our own health and of the children entrusted to our care. The wise old prophet Hosea cried out, "My people are destroyed for lack of knowledge" (Hosea 4:6). He may have been speaking in a different context, but the words are perfectly applicable to the destruction of human lives, the misery and heartache endured by countless millions. We take better care of our cars than our bodies. We insist upon preventive maintenance for these four-wheel chariots, but we shortchange our cells and fowl up our body metabolism. The insult to our tissues is nothing short of astonishing.

Dr. Karl Menninger, the famous psychiatrist from Topeka, Kansas, warned in his book *Whatever Became of Sin?* that we must regain our sense of sin so that we can obtain the peace of mind that we all desire. We must realize that we are sinning against our body when we injure it with the "enemy" foods.

When you disobey the laws of God with the way you treat your body, you are sinning and losing God's protection against the chronic degenerative diseases. You may rationalize and believe the propaganda of the food hierarchy, but it will not save you from the sins of your eating and drinking. Understand and believe that God wants the total you to live a life free from the dread diseases.

What Really Are Degenerative Diseases?

Degenerative means of, showing, or causing degeneration. When something degenerates it sinks below a former, normal, or higher quality of condition. In *biology* it means a gradual change to a lower form of development. In *medicine* it refers to biochemical change in tissues or organs, caused by injury or disease and leading to loss of vitality, function, etc.

Degenerative diseases are not caused by viruses, bacteria, or parasites, but by the body's inadequate metabolic response to a condition in which the cells of the body are being slowly poisoned by too many of the wrong things or by not getting enough of the right things at the right time. Enter arteriosclerotic vascular disease and its allied conditions, broadly referred to as heart disease, diabetes, cancer, arthritis, emphysema, hypoglycemia, and a number of other maladies—all reflections of the same underlying metabolic disorder.

The Greatest Single Killer in the World Today

It is a sobering fact that diseases of the heart and circulatory system claimed more American lives in 1974 than all other causes of death combined. This means that *more than one million people* died of this dread disease, or 54 percent of all deaths in that year. Broken down, the figures look like this:

665,000 from heart attacks
270,000 from strokes (the end product of high blood pressure and arteriosclerosis)
13,300 from rheumatic heart disease
19,000 from hypertensive disease
6,700 from congenital heart defects

Figures from that same year reveal that 30 million Americans had some major form of heart or circulatory disease, and that hypertension (high blood pressure) affected at least 24 million people, coronary heart disease another 4 million, rheumatic heart disease 1.8 million, and stroke 1.81 million.[2]

The Carnage from Heart Disease

We talk about the carnage of cancer, but the carnage from heart disease is equally disturbing, although the figures for heart disease are more difficult to come by. In sheer numbers alone, the effect is devastatingly alarming. Coronary disease is on the increase. More and more people, including younger people—people in the prime of life—are being struck down by heart attacks. We rightly ask "Why?" Basic principles for preventive measures have been put out by the American Heart Association, the National Heart Institute, and the American Medical Association. Head knowledge will not suffice. We deceive ourselves into believing "It only happens to the other fellow," and so we refuse to put into practice the proper preventive measures for ourselves.

Our apathy is sending us and our loved ones into early graves. Today there is even apathy about our apathy. Most Americans are too apathetic to be apathetic. I'm reminded of the story about the telephone survey conducted in an eastern state not long ago. The question was, "Do you think the greatest problem in America today is ignorance or apathy?" The major replies were, "I don't know" and "I don't care."

We must be willing to make a philosophical leap over the dedicated defendants of those who insist that things are not as bad as others of us would make them out to be. It is late—much later than most people think. There has been much misapplication of our scientific knowledge, thereby placing this country in the precarious position of hastening the premature development of breakdown diseases and the decline of our nation as a first-rate world power. There are those who once looked upon us as a forward-thinking, God-fearing nation, but who now regard us as a declining, decadent power.

The Lord of the universe spoke prophetic words to King Solomon which are often sounded as a means of reminding people to pray. We need to hear and heed them:

> If My people who are called by My name humble themselves and pray, and seek My face and turn from their wicked ways, then I will hear from heaven, will forgive their sin, and will heal their land.
>
> —2 Chronicles 7:14 NASB

I never detected in the dark days of the Depression the kind of spiritual desolation, the hypercritical cynicism, that devastates the lives of so many Americans today. We as a people are long overdue for a healing. The carnage of coronary disease includes hopeless, defeated, pessimistic attitudes that are pervasive. It seems that many Americans have lost what was once a characteristic optimism that formed the basis for an open-minded honesty and a willingness to confront the facts and then do something about them.

In dollar figures, what does heart disease cost? Again, these are statistics that are not easy to come by, but the cost has been estimated to be *at least* $27 billion per year (1974 statistics). That includes nearly $3 billion simply to pay physicians and nurses, $7 billion for hospitals and nursing homes, $700 million or more for heart medication, $1.1 billion to build the large hospital-research and surgical facilities, and a known $8.6 billion in lost wages.[3]

Time magazine's cover story of May 28, 1979, revealed that in 1978 more than 80,000 coronary bypass surgeries were performed, with an average cost of $10,000 to $15,000.

Intensive-care units account for about 15 percent of all hospital costs. Coronary-care units may charge $400 to $500 a day. Some doctors are not even sure whether survival rates are higher than would occur with care in regular hospital beds. Some physicians, according to the *Time* story, are concerned that the bright lights, alarms, and lack of privacy can frighten patients, impeding recovery or even precipitating fatal heart attacks.

Are these costs justified? Are all the procedures even necessary? Medicine has become an industry employing costly technology as sophisticated as that found in the space program, observes *Time*. Dr. William Anylan, vice president for health affairs at Duke University Medical Center in Durham, North Carolina, gives this example:

> Today, the patient with a heart problem sees his family practitioner who refers him to a nearby cardiologist, who then refers the patient to a tertiary center like Duke. He's evaluated by a clinical cardiologist, then goes to a group of diagnostic laboratory cardiologists and radiologists. If the patient is to be operated on, the surgeons, the anesthesiologist, the pump team, the blood bank in the institution that feeds the pump are involved. The patient goes to a special recovery room with specially trained people to watch him. He's there five days with round-the-clock care. He goes to a rehabilitation unit for the rest of his recovery.[4]

Soaring Bills

Health-care costs have the nation's decision-makers scratching their heads. Plainly, we are faced with a dilemma of catastrophic proportions. Even as this is being written, there is much legislative and political activity reflecting a pressing national concern. In 1965 the nation spent $38.9 billion in medical outlays of all kinds (hospital bills, physicians' fees, lab tests, etc.). That amounted to 5.9 percent of total spending for all goods and services. Since then, according to the *Time* magazine report, the bill has increased by 429 percent and in 1979 the total is expected to reach $206 billion, or 9.1 percent of the gross national product.

The White House has estimated that at this present rate of increase, medical costs will double every five years. That represents a rise far in excess of inflation. The economics of medicine have even doctors and hospital administrators admitting they are illogical. Rashi Fein, a noted Harvard medical economist, states: "Medicine is a social product like education. To ration health in terms of price is not the hallmark of a civilized society. You can differentiate between rich and poor with Cadillacs and yachts, but not with medicine.''[5]

We have been led to believe that these catastrophically inflationary costs are the inevitable side effect of good health. Statistics, however, do not reveal that we as a nation are that much more healthy!

Interestingly enough, the *Time* report states that many physicians argue that the only way the U.S. is going to bring its medical costs under control is by emphasizing preventive medicine instead of crisis care. ''They stress exercise, weight control, cutting out drinking and smoking.'' Dr. Hoyt D. Gardner, president-elect of the AMA is quoted as stating: ''America *medically* suffers more from affluence—and consequent self-indulgence—than from poverty.'' I would have to agree that his analysis is correct.

Too many Americans have the idea that one of the major roles of government is to take care of us from the womb to the tomb.

There are others who believe in living it up while the living is good, with little or no thought about the consequences to be suffered and paid later. ''I'm well insured,'' is their off-hand reply when reminded. What they fail to realize is that in the case of a major illness, their insurance coverage goes just so far. *The Tennessean Magazine* reports that sometimes the only solution to rising health care costs is bankruptcy. One Nashville attorney, a bankruptcy specialist, reports that ''medical costs are a major factor in well over 50 percent of bankruptcies.'' The magazine states that these are the people who are broken by the price tag of illness. They are the critical cases of what is becoming a national epidemic. Immunity is the refuge of the very few.[6]

Costs lose consequence in the face of crisis. And this is what the American public has been facing. In an emergency situation you don't shop around.

There is money in illness. Health-hunting Americans spend

more than $162 billion each year. Health care is this nation's third largest industry. It employs some 4.6 million people and is expected by some to take in nearly $230 billion by next year (1980).

Health care costs have been climbing twice as fast as the festering general inflation rate. . . . For a time that incision has been softened by the narcotic effect of a network of third-party payors: The Blues—Blue Shield and Blue Cross, private insurance policies, and government programs like Medicare and Medicaid.

Now, however, even those who fluff these bill-paying pillows are starting to look hard at what they're ladling out to physicians, hospitals and others. As payments rise, premiums do too, whether paid by employers, employees or taxes.

"The circle is very complete, we are all in it," a Washington, D.C.-based businessman told a health cost conference. . . .7

Stop the World, I Want to Get Off. But Tell Me How!

How does one get off this merry-go-round? It's true that most of us see a doctor when we're bleeding and hurting—seldom before. And we recognize that doctors put in long years preparing and studying to become "angels of healing," as it were. We know, too, that they put in long hours and much overtime, and that they are almost always on call. The Tennessee Medical Association (TMA), in a brochure entitled *Why Medical Costs Have Increased,* points out that "physicians receive only 18.6% of the dollars expended on health care, which is a lower percentage than five years ago." The average physician works a 60-hour week and earns slightly more than $60,000 a year (according to TMA's executive director). The demands from patients and the community on the doctor's time, energy, and wallet are higher than on the average businessman.

Thomas Edison is credited with saying, "The doctor of the future will give no medicine but will interest his patients in the care of the human frame, in diet, and in the cause and prevention of disease." It would appear that we are a long way from reaching that desired place.

The Chronic Killers

Modern metabolic medicine's thinking leads me to conclude that our chronically sick state is due to what I call "hypocellulosis"—a word you were introduced to in a previous chapter. In hypocellulosis you will find a state of sick cells. The lessened activity of these sick cells brings about impaired, below-par cell metabolism, and we become *hypometabolic*. These sick cells, unable to metabolize efficiently, cannot rid themselves of all the end products of poor metabolism, and we have a cell state that I call *cell pollution*.

We can see air pollution because we can look out the window and view the "smaze" (smog and haze) in our environment, but unfortunately we do not think about the excessive cellular debris that collects in our cells. It should be evident that if the body doesn't rid itself of all its end products, then we'll suffer the ill effects of this cell "garbage" which furthers the many conditions we point to as chronic disease.

Hypoglycemia

Hypoglycemia is, I believe, an early chronic breakdown disease which is the precursor of a number of other degenerative diseases. *Hypoglycemia* is a word composed of two parts: *Hypo,* or "low," and *glycemia,* or glucose—so hypoglycemia means low blood sugar.

The term was first employed by Dr. Seale Harris in 1924. He considered hypoglycemia as a condition in which the patient had low blood sugar due to too much insulin; so he used the terms *hyperinsulinism* and *hypoglycemia* interchangeably. These terms continued to be used interchangeably until my book *Nutrigenetics* was published in 1975. My book demonstrated that hypoglycemia is always the forerunner of diabetes, and may lead to heart disease, stroke, liver, and kidney disorders, and other serious degenerative diseases.

As pointed out in that book, hypoglycemia is caused when an individual who suffers from a specific genetic weakness fails to strengthen it with nutritious eating. Thus the use of the word *nutrigenetics*—a combined form of nutritive and genetic influences.

Fortunately, more people today are learning about the ravages of hypoglycemia. More of us have begun to realize that the average American gets too many processed carbohydrates, too much saturated fat, and too little usable protein.

The Seale Harris diet for hypoglycemia was based on the theory that a person should eat more frequently to help maintain a more stable blood-sugar level. This is still considered a proper basis for treating some blood-sugar symptoms. However, *Nutrigenetics* was one of the first books to mention that the body needs many things to help utilize nutrients in every food intake. I recommend that concentrated nutrients be added to most persons' deficient reserves.

Anyone who has a tendency toward blood-sugar problems must become thoroughly informed about what is in food and what must be added to good food to promote and maintain good heath—and, incidentally, to keep himself happy for life.

A Mother's Lament

I was shocked when I read a letter from Mrs. B. The letter concerned her son, Duke, who first came to me as a patient when he was 24. "Duke died August 8," she wrote. He and his little family has gone to Colorado for their annual vacation. He had a heart attack and was in the hospital. He was doing fine, so his doctor thought, and was going to be released August 29. Instead, Duke died from a heart attack at age 29.

It had been five years since I'd seen Duke. He was overweight and his blood-fat levels were high, as were his blood sugar. Duke showed considerable improvement over a period of several months as he cooperated with me. He talked much about weight loss, but I explained to him that what we were really trying to do was to prevent his having a heart attack at an early age.

To me it was far more important to be concerned about the fat within the walls of his arteries than to spend so much time worrying about the fat deposits beneath his skin. After a few more visits Duke did not return, and his mother explained that he did not have the time or the money to come back for continuing treatment. (I learned via the "grapevine," however, that Duke had enough time and money to go fishing in his new $3500 boat.)

The story of Duke is typical of many of our young men today. The death rate of bright and promising junior executives is increasing at an alarming rate. These fellows are fatally stricken when they are still in their twenties, thirties, and forties. The report of Duke further supports my conviction for the urgent need to practice preventive medicine on a wider and more conscientious level.

Predictive Medicine

Along with the importance of preventive practice is the importance of *predictive medicine*. The value of predictive medicine is now established. Predictive medicine indicates the presence of conditions or factors which increase the patient's susceptibility and show the disposition toward certain diseases and disorders.

Predictive medicine is especially valuable because it focuses our attention on the prevalence of products of abnormal metabolic processes. This condition is the forerunner of artery disease and coronary attacks (which are really arterial).

A statement for physicians in the AMA pamphlet entitled "Risk Factors and Coronary Disease" reports that coronary attack proneness is usually identified with one or more of the following indicators: elevated levels of cholesterol or triglycerides, elevated blood-pressure readings, obesity, elevated blood sugar levels, and higher-than-normal uric acid. They failed to include low blood-sugar levels, which should be named as an early chronic degenerative disease and indicator of future artery disease. These evidences of abnormal metabolism can be likened to the carbon deposits which occur in your car when the gasoline vapor does not burn completely in the combustion chamber.

Hypoglycemia and Cardiovascular Disease

Low blood-sugar levels are often the final insult to a weakened heart that has long been starved by clogged arteries. Many heart attacks occur several hours after the victim has eaten a large meal. Authorities believe that the attacks are precipitated by low blood sugar. A sudden lowering of the blood sugar which may occur in the hypoglycemic, normal, or hyperglycemic range was observed to precipitate objective signs of cardiac damage. Elimination of these episodes by employing a low-carbohydrate, high-protein diet reportedly controlled the anginal attacks. [8]

It has also been observed that persons with peripheral arterial disease, or who had experienced a first myocardial infarction, consumed significant amounts of sugar. International statistics show that countries with increased sugar consumption also show an increase in the heart-disease death rate.

Low blood sugar—hypoglycemia—is very definitely the precursor state or "early warning system" for a whole host of interlocking degenerative diseases. Dr. Harold W. Harper, in *How You Can Beat the Killer Diseases,* emphasizes that hypoglycemia is rarely diagnosed until it is well on its way to becoming something more serious, but the symptoms would not be ignored, for they are frequently the early-warning signs of eventual diabetes, arthritis, arteriosclerosis, and even cancer. The medical world has ambivalent views about hypoglycemia and often will not administer the proper six-hour glucose-tolerance test which will indicate whether a person has glucose metabolism dysfunction (GMD) or not.

According to Dr. Harper:

The importance of discovering and treating hypoglycemia can be seen in the following statistics: 80 percent of untreated hypoglycemics will eventually end up diabetics. In addition, a significant number of diabetics also develop cancer. And by the time arteriosclerosis is diagnosed, the "sugar junkie" is apt to be well on the way to death from heart disease.[9]

The sooner we acknowledge that learning to understand one's metabolism and working to keep metabolic balance is the key to prevention of degenerative diseases, the more likely will be your success in preservation and maintenance of optimum health.

This book is concerned primarily with cancer and coronary disease. You don't have to fear either of these diseases and their related companions if you take the *proper* precautions and exercise discipline and discernment. The choice is up to you.

The Apostle John, writing to his dear friend Gaius many years ago, expressed it so well:

> Dear friend, I pray that you may enjoy good health and that all may go well with you, even as your soul is getting along well (III John 2).

That is my sincere wish for you too.

FOOTNOTES

1. Harold W. Harper, M.D., and Michael L. Culbert, *How You Can Beat the Killer Diseases* (New Rochelle, N.Y.: Arlington House, 1977), p. 50.
2. Ibid., p. 49.
3. Ibid., p. 49.
4. "Health Costs: What Limit?" in *Time* magazine, May 28, 1979, p. 64.
5. Ibid., p. 66.
6. "What to Do About the Cost of Health?" in *The Tennessean* magazine, May 1979, p. 15.
7. Ibid., p. 16.
8. Cheraskin and Ringdorf, *Diet & Disease* (Emmaus, Penna.: Rodale Books, n.d.), p. 264.
9. Harper, p. 58.

6

It has become increasingly
clear that the first line of
defense is the informed
patient and his family. If
the individual does not
understand how to preserve
health and recognize when
help is needed, and is
prepared to take steps to
obtain help, all the world's
medical knowledge is of
little value.
—Dr. Irving S. Wright,
Chairman of the Inter-
Society Commission for
Heart Disease Resources

The What and Why
Of Coronary Disease

Not much bigger than your clenched fist, your heart is a mighty little organ! So far, no machine has been invented to take the heart's place. The heart remains, therefore, our most vital organ.

The late heart-specialist Dr. Paul Dudley White called coronary heart disease "one of the largest epidemics in medical history." Heart disease is rightly called "Public Enemy Number One." It is the leading cause of death in white males 35 and older, the leading cause of death in black males 30 and over, the leading cause of death in black women 35 and over, and the leading cause of death in white women 40 and over. Arteriosclerotic vascular disease is so widespread and growing so rapidly in incidence that it is far from being the disease of any one age group or nationality of people. Even infants and young children die of coronary artery disease! Autopsies of infants and young children indicate that calcium deposits in the arteries of these children brought about their untimely death. This happened because the mother ingested abnormal nutrients and vitamin D2 during pregnancy, and they crossed the placenta during the gestation period.

Calcium deposited at abnormal places in the body of anyone—regardless of age or race—will lead to the formation of arteriosclerotic plaques on a fatty matrix (the substance between the cells of tissue). (Calcium is the primary mineral component of most arteriosclerotic plaques.)

But coronary heart disease is not something that just suddenly happens to us. Captain George L. Calvy, director of the Medical Field Research Laboratory in Camp Lejeune, North Carolina, wrote: ''. . . coronary heart disease has an incubation period just as do the well-known childhood infectious diseases mumps and measles. . . . In the case of coronary heart disease, the incubation period may be 10 to 20 years.''

We start dying the moment we are born. Why? Because malnutrition at the cellular level is so widespread, and this is the spot—the cells—where illness begins and we start aging. Longevity is dependent upon freedom from disease, much of which is dietary in origin. Dr. White urged that the public be educated as to what it is that contributes to these degenerative diseases, particularly coronary and cerebral atherosclerosis and thrombosis.

Nearly all of today's youth suffer from malnutrition at the cellular level. Health does not come by chance; it is the result of obedience to divine law. The Bible has many references, direct and indirect, which warn against intemperance in eating. Medical science has been speaking for generations to the need for guarding one's health. Too many people are content to sit on the sidelines and blame everyone but themselves for the diseases that end up ravaging their bodies. We might compare this attitude to the horse and the barn door. We have a tendency to close the door after our health has escaped! To stand at the drugstore counter and try to buy good health with a doctor's prescription in your hand is an all-too-common sight.

What Early Medical Practitioners Had to Say

Nutrition and one's eating habits are vital to one's state of health. In fact, the role of nutrition in the very early medical practices was not overlooked. Hippocrates wrote:

> For the art of medicine would not have been invented at first, nor would it have been made a subject of investigation (for there would be no need of it), if when men are indisposed, the same food and other articles of regimen which they eat and drink when in good health, were proper for them, and if no others were preferable to these.

Celsus, often called the Roman Hippocrates, wrote this in one of his eight books on medicine:

> After having spoken of those things which benefit by depleting, we come to those which nourish, namely food and drink. Now these are of general assistance not only in diseases of all kinds but in preserving health as well; and an acquaintance with the properties of all is of importance, in the first place that those in health may know how to make use of them, then, as we follow on to the treatment of disease, we can state the species of ailments to be consumed. . . .

One major factor in the medical profession's failure to retain the wisdom of Hippocratic aphorisms was the embracing of the germ theory of disease as advanced by Louis Pasteur's dramatic discoveries which showed that microbes cause disease.

The germ theory of disease, of course, advanced and accelerated the idea of specific causes of disease but failed to retain the basic fact that immune processes of the body are basic factors in preventing disease problems.

The Two Basic Problems Concerning the Human Diet

Today we have two problems concerning the human diet—undereating and overeating. These problems are not necessarily the result of one's economic status; the very wealthy can be just as undernourished through bad dietary judgment or neglect, simply because they can afford the best of everything and tend to spend much on food and drink. In either case the effects on the state of health can be serious and often irreversible. The ever-increasing occurrence of cardiovascular diseases seems to be found among the affluent peoples privileged to live in this "land of plenty" of ours.

Nutritional biochemistry can no longer be considered by the medical student or the physician as a dispensable and esoteric subject. It provides the disciplinary base for an increasing number of diagnostic, therapeutic, and preventive procedures in the practice of medicine. Considering the fact that the heart is a muscle in constant motion for as long as you live, it, above all, needs a ready supply of nutrients for the metabolic machinery necessary to transform into energy to keep this muscle pumping at a regular rate. Since energy is transformed from the carbohydrates in food, all nutrients are essential for a healthy heart. But the carbohydrate source should come from something other than sugar because the ingestion of refined sugar forms carbonic acid, which interferes with the smooth and rhythmic function of the blood and of the heart.

What About One's Ancestors?

I can hear them now, the questions, objections, and defensive arguments the reader will raise at this point. "I'm not going to worry about statistics. My family and my husband's (or wife's) family are of good, hardy stock. Why, granddad never had a sick day in his life and he lived past 90. And the members on the other side of the family lived the good life with plenty of fat meat and rich foods. Their only complaint was occasional indigestion!"

Let's look at the daily habits and routines of these people just mentioned. Did they have a car? Did the kids travel to school by bus? Were the garden fruits and vegetables purchased at the supermarket in frozen form? Was the meat supply stocked in the local frozen-food locker? And what did they do for recreation? Did they eat 170 pounds of sugar a year? Did they eat processed cereal and bakery products?

After you have tallied your answers to these questions, consider your own way of life now. Quite a difference, isn't there?

Physical Activity and the Kinds of Food Do Matter

The automobile did not become a family luxury until the 1920s. Walking was not considered undignified, and the entire family covered a lot of miles on foot getting to and from school, church, friends, and relatives.

If your grandparents didn't live on a farm and butcher their own meat, then chances are they kept a few chickens penned up in the backyard. Other relatives and/or friends may have contributed to their sources of meat and fowl. And the garden! I'll bet you pulled many a carrot and dug a few potatoes for the dinner table at Grandma's house. One of my most pleasant childhood memories is that of stopping in the middle of play to run to the garden, pull up some radishes and carrots, stop at the cistern (which we had to prime) to wash them off, and then to happily munch on them. How many children in our urban areas are able to do that today?

Summing it all up, this "hardy stock" of which you are so proud got that way through plenty of exercise and fresh air. Convenience cooking and labor-saving devices are a quite recent blight on the American scene. Our much-touted "leisure time to enjoy life" has developed a culture of overweight and undernourished Americans getting their kicks and vicarious thrills from sitting in front of the TV or in the sports stadium. While these same people are sitting around being entertained, they are consuming vast quantities of sweets, liquor, beer, nuts, and popcorn. Then at mealtime a "better" diet is usually prepared and presented. But what is to become of the accumulated fats and carbohydrates, especially from the junk-food snacks, that are not being used up by the body through normal muscular work and exercise? They begin to deposit here and there throughout the tissues, and slowly a build up of fats collects in the circulatory system, narrowing the channels of flow for the blood.

As the walls of these arterial tubules become thicker, the blood has less room to travel and the heart must work harder to push the blood through the system around the body. Eventually these arteries will either close up with fat deposits (myocardial infarction) or the arterial walls will lose their elasticity when cholesterol accumulates (hardening of the arteries, or atherosclerosis), and a heart attack will result.

That Mighty Little Organ

What really is the heart? The human heart is a four-chambered, tough, hollow muscle. An electrically fired pumping machine, it alternately squeezes and relaxes in a closed system of flexible pipes, keeping fluids within the pipes in constant circulation. The blood is kept on a constant circular journey by means of this muscle. The journey is dual, with every drop of blood following first one circuit and then the other. The first is a short circuit—from the right side of the heart, through the lungs to collect oxygen and back to the left side of the heart.

In the second journey a major trip is involved as the blood is pumped from the left side of the heart throughout every part of the body and back to the right side of the heart. In the course of this second journey the blood gives up its oxygen to the tissues.

How Important Is Oxygen?

Oxygen is vital. The blood is merely the vehicle which carries oxygen and other important supplies to the tissues, with the heart acting as the machine carrying out the essential function of propelling the blood. All of this is interrelated and is of tremendous importance. William Harvey (1578-1657), the discoverer of circulation, rather despairingly concluded that "The motion of the heart was to be comprehended only by God."

The great nerve centers which control our heartbeats, our breathing, and our other vital processes must have a constant supply of fresh blood that is rich in oxygen. When the percentage of oxygen in the blood falls, respiration is stimulated and we breathe deeper and more rapidly. The heart therefore is stimulated to beat faster whenever the body demands an increased supply of oxygen or fuel for any reason. Any impairment in the pulmonary circulation system places an extra burden on the heart muscle. It is impossible to exaggerate the importance of the circulation through the coronary arteries. Obstruction to the flow of blood through these arteries or their branches may result in damage to the muscular walls of the heart.

You are familiar with the words *coronary thrombosis*. The word "thrombosis" means the formation of blood-clots, which can occur in any blood vessel in the body. When this happens, doctors call it "a coronary." Actually, "coronary" is the name given to two vitally important arteries. Because they are the first branches leaving the aorta, they arise very close to its root and therefore contain blood which is particularly rich in oxygen.

The coronary arteries are the arteries which supply the walls of the heart muscle itself with blood. These arteries branch repeatedly so that tiny twigs, as it were, carry oxygen and nourishment to every single muscle fiber of the heart.

Although there is great variability from person to person, for convenience sake let's say that the heart contracts and expands about 72 to 75 times per minute, or over 100,000 times a day, or nearly 38 million times a year! If you live out your biblical quota of 70 years, your heart will beat over 2½ billion times without stopping! If you are an average-sized adult, your heart will pump between 2500 and 3500 gallons of blood each 24 hours. Each heartbeat pumps about four ounces of blood with each contraction. Heart function is so important that about 1/20 of that blood goes through the coronary arteries to supply the heart itself.

A Look at Vitamin E

Wilfrid E. Shute and his older brother, Evan, have been investigating the medical and physiological properties of vitamin E and utilizing this vitamin (which is little-known to many doctors) in their extensive practices. What their research and efforts offer is hope for ailing and healthy hearts. The Shute brothers are of the opinion that when new and "more efficient" milling methods were introduced into the manufacture of wheat flour, those methods permitted the complete stripping away of the highly perishable wheat germ, and the diet of Western man lost its only significant source of vitamin E. Flour milling underwent this great change around the turn of the century, and it became general around 1910. The amount of vitamin E in the diet was greatly reduced, and with the loss of this natural antithrombin, coronary thrombosis appeared on the scene.[1]

This more than anything else, these brothers believe, explains our present mortality rate for heart disease. It must be remembered that coronary thrombosis was unknown as a disease entity in 1900 and apparently hardly existed at that time. It wasn't until 1912 that six cases were reported in Chicago and medical practitioners began to be aware of coronary thrombosis as a possibility. Dr. Paul Dudley White said that when he graduated from medical school in 1911 he had never heard of coronary thrombosis. He called that disease "one of the chief threats to life in the United States and Canada," and concluded that for this to happen in one's own lifetime was "an astonishing development" and that "There can be no doubt but that coronary heart disease has reached epidemic proportions in the United States, where it is now responsible for more than 50 percent of all deaths. . . ."

The Shute brothers' interest in vitamin E began in 1933 and continues to the present time. Extensive experimentation and work with cardiac patients has proven that alpha tocopherol (vitamin E) is a thoroughly tried and tested therapeutic agent, unusually successful in its results and with its effects so well-defined that it can be used with precision by any competent physician.[2]

Digitalis, a medicine made from plants of the figwort family (foxglove), has long been used as a heart stimulant. Alpha tocopherol has an action similar to that of digitalis on the hypoxic (oxygen-deficient) heart. Can the two be used together? To most scientists, vitamin E and alpha tocopherol are the same substance, but alpha tocopherol is one of six tocopherols found in the vitamin itself. Actually the strength of vitamin E preparations is rated pharmacologically in terms of their alpha tocopherol content. The answer to the question is that vitamin E (alpha tocopherol) is a vitamin, and yes, any digitalis given a heart patient is even more effective when the patient is on alpha tocopherol. In most cases, the dosage of digitalis used should be no more than half of the usual therapeutic dose, and it may be much less.[3]

There are virtually only three commonly used drugs which are known to be incompatible with alpha tocopherol—inorganic iron, mineral oil, and female sex hormones. The Shute book recommends that the patient take all his alpha tocopherol in one dose and the other drugs (if used) 12 hours later.

Nitroglycerine, the antihypertensive drugs, and diuretics can safely be used as adjunct therapy along with alpha tocopherol.

Anyone who has had a coronary occlusion, or has seen a family member suffer from this, knows that in many cases the patient can develop intense chest pain known as angina pectoris. Often, angina pectoris will precede the onset of the so-called attack. Angina develops gradually due to narrowing of the coronary arteries and the consequent diminishing of the blood supply to the heart muscle—the myocardium. It has been proven in thousands of cases that the action of alpha tocopherol diminishes and relieves these painful symptoms. Of course, many factors are involved because of the variations in people. What this indicates, however, is that vitamin E is a biological antioxidant. Alpha tocopherol reduces oxygen need, and thereby increases tolerance and prevents premature and undesirable oxidation of lipids (fats and other substances of similar properties) in the bloodstream. It keeps available to the tissues a higher proportion of the oxygen taken into the blood.

Its second action of major importance relates to its ability to dissolve fresh thrombi (coagulation of the blood in some part of the circulatory system, forming a clot that obstructs circulation in that part) and to prevent the occurrence of thrombosis. A patient who has suffered from the results of a previous thrombosis would be particularly benefited by the regular taking of vitamin E.

The benefits of vitamin E can hardly be overstated. I particularly urge the reader to obtain and study the Shute book entitled *Vitamin E for Ailing and Healthy Hearts*. It is good to know that there is no danger of toxicity with alpha tocopherol treatment.

What About the Blood Itself?

How is it possible for this red fluid in your body to accomplish so many vital tasks? First of all, your five quarts of blood are composed of some 30 trillion cells, which in turn fall into three basic types—red cells (erythrocytes), white cells (leucocytes), and platelets (thrombocytes). Of these three types, the red blood cells are the principal carriers of oxygen and the nutrients needed by the cells, as well as the carbon dioxide and other waste products. Your body makes about 150 million new red blood cells in the bone marrow every day during your lifetime (26 million new red cells every second to replace the equal number of old and useless red cells which are destroyed by the liver and the spleen). The function of the white cells is to attack invading bacteria, while the platelets are involved in the clotting reaction.

If we were to follow one of these blood cells on a single round trip in the circulatory system (from the heart to the lungs, back to the heart, throughout the body, and again back to the heart), the entire circuit would take only 23 to 30 seconds, or about 27 heartbeats. This means that a single cell may make about 3000 trips a day through the circulatory system of the human body.

What Determines the Regularity of the Heartbeat?

The oxygen which we inhale combines (in the system) with carbon present in the food we eat, forming CO_2 (carbon dioxide), which dissolves in the body liquids as a very weak acid, H_2CO_3 (carbonic acid), and the heartbeat is regulated by the carbonic acid content of the blood.

The carbon dioxide, carried as a waste product by the red blood cells and exhaled in our breath, results from the chemical breakdown of glucose, a simple sugar, found in many foods. This glucose molecule ($C_6H_{12}O_6$) breaks apart during the energy-extraction cycle to become carbon dioxide and water.

With all of these factors in mind, one can readily understand both the ensuing problems created by abnormal metabolism imbalance and the risk of allowing these problems to go unattended.

Dr. Christiaan Barnard, a name quickly recognized for performing the first human heart transplant in history in Cape Town, South Africa, on December 3, 1967, made the statement, "I am convinced that either a mechanical heart or a transplanted heart is the answer to heart problems." That is not what our Creator intended!

Myocardial Infarction

Artery disease is better known in medical circles by the term *myocardial infarction* (tissue destruction in the heart). Modern concern about coronary artery diseases developed after Dr. Adam Hammer diagnosed the condition in a living patient about a hundred years ago. It has now assumed the role of the great "Modern Epidemic," according to the late eminent heart specialist, Dr. Paul Dudley White.

We have already shown you what can happen when blockage by a clot in a small coronary artery within the heart muscle develops. Deprived of its nourishing blood supply, that particular area of the heart will die and its function of contracting will cease. For those who recover, the damaged area will be replaced by scar tissue. Myocardial infarction is currently the most common cause of death in the United States. It is a consequence of, and usually associated with, generalized atherosclerosis.

Each year more than a million heart attacks are recorded in this country, with 600,000 deaths due to coronary heart disease. One-and-a-half percent of these attacks occur in the "under 65" age group. Sixty percent of all patients who develop an acute myocardial infarction die before they reach the intensive care unit at the hospital. A postmortem study of 350 patients at the Massachusetts General Hospital who died of various diseases revealed that all had evidence of coronary artery disease. The problem seems to be universal, and if you are an American it is not the question of *if* you have artery disease, but rather *how serious* the disease may be, and which arteries are most dangerously involved.

In contrast to the above study, a similar group study in southern Japan showed a good many people with smooth-walled, normal arteries. This frightening contrast shows that we can no longer be indifferent to the casual relationship between abnormal metabolism and unhealthy arteries.

Most Heart Attacks Are Caused by Atherosclerosis

You have no doubt heard the term *atherosclerosis* before reading this book, and we have mentioned the word several times in this and the preceding chapter. Let's look at it in a bit more detail.

Atherosclerosis is a derivative of *arteriosclerosis,* a thickening and hardening of the walls of the arteries that is often associated with old age. That, however, is a false assumption, as is being proved more and more with the untimely deaths of men and women in midlife or earlier. *Atherosclerosis* is a tumor filled with grainy matter, arteriosclerosis in which the inmost wall of the artery undergoes fatty degeneration.

Over the years the blood carries various nutrients to all parts of the body, causing it to grow and develop. However, at some point along the way the arteries fail to handle certain elements in the blood, and large amounts of lipids (blood fats, cholesterol, and triglycerides) accumulate as part of the fatty deposits on the artery walls. Since the chemical makeup and distribution of the lipids in the atheroma closely resemble the lipids in the serum of the blood, it is felt that the blood fats tend to deposit on the vessel walls.

Fat deposits in the walls of the large arteries can be seen in most young adults. This unhealthy state progresses to the calcified and ulcerated conditions found in medium and large arteries of later life. This sets the stage for heart attacks and strokes at a time when a person should be ready to relax and enjoy life.

Angina Pectoris

Angina pectoris is heart condition in which there are spasms of pain in the chest, with feelings of suffocation, usually due to anemia of the heart muscle. Typically, an attack of angina is described by the patient as a sensation of pressure, tightness, or heaviness behind the breastbone. It may become crushing in nature, like a closing vise, and may be very severe indeed. It can come on so suddenly that it seems instantaneous, with the victim suddenly subjected to unbearable pain that renders him unable even to walk. The attack can end quickly or can continue until it is treated. The pain has a tendency to radiate, usually to the left shoulder and arm and all the way down to the fingers. It is often accompanied by great anxiety and a fear of impending death.[4]

It now goes almost unquestioned that angina is caused by oxygen lack. This points up the need, as many doctors recognize now, for utilization of alpha tocopherol (vitamin E) as the ideal therapy. It is also important to use vitamin E preventively as a regular part of one's "nutrition-plus" program. What vitamin E does is to bond with the fatty acids and prevent their oxidation. How much easier it would be to the person troubled with angina to take a few vitamin E capsules daily, thus preventing the recurrence of angina attacks in most cases, and not have to rely upon the drug nitroglycerin!

Dr. Shute believes strongly, as others of us do, that the time has come to point out that the average cardiologist can do nothing to help a damaged heart *if he does not use vitamin E.* All he can do is to treat symptoms and complications.

High Blood Pressure (Hypertension)

High blood pressure and hypertension—the two are synonymous in most people's thinking. High blood pressure is considered by the medical profession to be the "silent killer," contributing in a major way to heart attacks and strokes.

The reason for this, of course, is that you can have high blood pressure—even at what would be considered fairly elevated levels—and feel perfectly well.

The question is often asked, "What is considered normal blood pressure?" The nurse comes in and wraps the sleeve around your arm. She's going to check your blood pressure. There will be the systolic and the diastolic readings. The first is the upper level of blood pressure (the pressure which exists within your arteries at the moment when your heart is pumping out the blood). Diastolic blood pressure is the lower pressure within the arteries—the baseline just before the next heartbeat.

You've no doubt heard it said that the normal systolic blood pressure is 100 plus your age. The World Health Organization defines hypertension as anything higher than 160 over 95. Recent studies show that 160 over 100, or even 150 over 90, definitely *increases* the risk of heart attacks and strokes. Insurance company statistics involving several hundred thousand people clearly show that above a blood pressure of 140 over 90, the incidence of heart attacks begins to increase. Normal would be considered 140 over 85 but it can fluctuate greatly with age, occupation, and many other variables.

New evidence indicates that even mild elevations of blood pressure are potentially harmful, particularly where other risk factors are also present, such as diabetes, a moderately elevated cholesterol, recurrent headaches, throbbing, palpitations, or dizziness. Any of these symptoms warrant examination. All studies, both in man and animals, show that the effects of high blood pressure and high cholesterol are geometrically related in their harmful effect on the body. The risk of heart attack is increased three to five times if both are present.

Early treatment of young and middle-aged individuals is well advised; clinically, elderly people who have a mild elevation of systolic pressure (perhaps 180 to 190) may not require treatment.

Untreated high blood pressure is like playing a prolonged game of Russian roulette.

What Causes High Blood Pressure?

When we talk about causes of this "silent killer," we have to admit that we don't know the exact cause for many people.

Stress certainly contributes to an elevation of blood pressure, particularly over an extended period of time. The work habits of many men and women have forced them into the role of being workaholics.

Clinical observation has revealed that the mechanism of essential hypertension in human beings involves the kidneys and their role in eliminating dietary salt. The person genetically predisposed to high blood pressure does not handle excessive salt well. The kidney retains the excess dietary salt, which in turn affects the volume of the blood plasma and of the extracellular fluid in the body. Intricate biochemical mechanisms are involved that lead to high blood pressure.

Preventive-minded doctors tell you to cut down (or cut out) salt and meat intake and increase vitamin C and zinc intake, and you'll be on the road to a less pressured life. According to Dr. William B. Kannel, director of the famous Framingham Heart Study in Massachusetts, "Dozens of drugs are available to lower blood pressure, but now when most doctors—and patients—talk about hypertension, the first thing they think of is pills, not behavioral changes."

So the high-blood pressure victim, pops a pill into his mouth which will help his body shed excess salt—and may drive up his blood pressure. Ironically, the same diuretic responsible for washing away excess salt may drain the body of potassium as well. And potassium is an important mineral necessary for the functioning of many body tissues, including the heart. Fortunately, this drawback can be overcome with potassium supplements (if your doctor alerts you to this necessity) or by requesting special "potassium-sparing" diuretics from your physician.

But everyone reacts differently to medication; other complications may result from continued use of diuretics—i.e., depression, impotence, dizziness, headache, insomnia, muscle weakness, nausea, diarrhea, palpitations, and blindness. Diuretics also tend to wash out the water-soluble vitamins and minerals as well. There is also evidence now that for many people blood pressure medication may not be giving them the protection they think it is. According to a study appearing in the *American Journal of Medicine* (November 1976), diuretics may lower your blood pressure, but they do not necessarily reduce your chance of heart attack.[5]

Diet Therapy Is a Better Solution

The use of diuretics may increase the level of cholesterol by an average of 11 milligrams per 100 milliliters of blood, and the triglyceride level by approximately 34 milligrams per 100 milliliter.[6] This was demonstrated in a test involving 39 patients with mild hypertension.

Pressure went down but cholesterol went up. Is that the risk one wishes to take? Thirty-five participants in this same study showed a satisfactory reduction in high-blood-pressure levels with *diet therapy alone.*

Studies of the Greenland Eskimos, the Melanesian tribesmen in New Guinea and the Solomon Islands, the Easter Islanders, the Australian Aborigines, the Congo Pygmies, and the Bushmen of the Kalahari Desert all reveal one common denominator which binds all these primitive people together—lack of added salt in the diet. Among all these groups you will find very little incidence of high blood pressure. In contrast, the average American consumes 7 to 15 grams of salt per day (close to three teaspoons), according to the *Journal of the American Medical Association* (March 8, 1977).

We might list the factors influencing blood pressure like this:

HARMFUL	BENEFICIAL	
salt		
meat	low-salt diets	exercise
tension	raw foods	garlic
cigarettes	relaxation	zinc
alcohol		
	vitamin C	

A return to the biblical basics is called for. From early culture, man was a gatherer of nuts and berries long before he became a hunter. It was God's original plan to keep man well by eating right.

Vegetarians, it can be shown, have the edge on heart disease. A high potassium intake is advisable for anyone with potential hypertension. This can be obtained from foods such as bananas, raisins, prunes, tomato juice, fruit juices, and melons. Salt levels are high in milk products and processed meats. Baby foods also contain much salt, and, tragically, high blood pressure is not uncommon in children, as was formerly believed.

High blood pressure is not a disease, but it is an abnormality. It may be a sign of disease, but it can also stand alone. Not everyone who suffers from a raised blood pressure is suffering from hypertension; some people have a "labile" blood pressure (one that is raised only intermittently).

A well-known doctor who suffered from angina in the eighteenth century is credited with saying, "My life is at the mercy of any knave who cares to annoy me."

Congenital Heart Disease

There is another kind of heart problem that is by no means rare. Congenital heart disease has to do with babies born with structural defects of the heart. It is felt that approximately 25,000 babies are born yearly with abnormal hearts in the U.S. alone. Vast forward leaps in cardiac surgery in recent years have brought new hope to the parents of such children, and in many instances have brought restored life.

Chronic Rheumatic Heart Disease

This is the second-most-common form of heart disease, and it accounts for 30 percent of the crippled hearts in the adult. It causes death in 30,000 to 60,000 persons annually in the U.S. It accounts for virtually all heart-disease deaths between the age of 5 and 25 years, and 50 percent of all deaths before the age of 30.

Dr. Shute has had great success in treating victims of rheumatic heart disease with vitamin E (alpha tocopherol). (See details in his book *Vitamin E for Ailing and Healthy Hearts.*)

The incidence of rheumatic fever (and consequently of the patient developing rheumatic heart disease) has been decreasing since the sulfonamide and antibiotic era of drugs has come on the scene. There are still those people, however, who had their acute attacks of rheumatic fever before the antibiotic era, and these people who today are suffering from chronic rheumatic heart disease. There are no accurate statistics available, but it has been suggested that 1 to 6 percent of the general population may have specific rheumatic valvular defects.

Strokes

More than 1.8 million people have strokes every year in this country. From that number, more than 270,000 die from these strokes. Warning signs are unusual; usually the suddenness of a stroke gives little time for warning signals. But these are the signs that a stroke may be occurring:

1. Temporary weakness or numbness of the face, arms, or legs.
2. A temporary loss of speech, or difficulty in word association and in completing sentences.
3. Temporary blindness or diminution of vision, usually in one eye rather than both.
4. Episodes of double vision.
5. Unexplained dizziness or unsteadiness.

Are there things one can do to avoid the possibility of a stroke? Many fatal strokes could be prevented by properly taking care of the hypertension that preceded them. More than 10 percent of the American population (about 24 million people) are hypertensive.

Of that number, these figures are significant:

Half of those who have the problem don't know it (the "silent killer" aptly named).

25 percent of those who do know they have it are not doing anything about it.

The remaining 25 percent know they have it and are trying to do something about it.

Of this 25 percent, 12.5 percent are having success in controlling it.

Prevention

More will be said on preventive measures in succeeding chapters, but we will conclude this chapter by emphasizing the following:

1. A change in lifestyle that includes a nutritional program and an adequate exercise program.

2. The possibility of chelation therapy as an alternative to surgery. (More in chapter 12.)

3. Elimination of stress as much as possible.

4. Avoidance of contamination with vaporized chemicals and heavy metals. When unavoidable, wear a mask.

5. Discontinuance of smoking and drinking.

6. Regular examinations by your doctor (preferably a physician who believes in preventive measures such as outlined in this and other books recommended throughout this book.

7. A program of therapeutic augmentation through the use of concentrated nutrients.

8. Peace with God and your fellowman.

FOOTNOTES

1. Wilfrid E. Shute, M.D. with Harald J. Taub, *Vitamin E for Ailing & Healthy Hearts* (Denver: The Nutri-Books Corp., 1969), pp. 11, 12.
2. Ibid., p. 17.
3. Ibid., p. 18.
4. Ibid., p. 43.
5. *Prevention* magazine, August 1977, p. 92.
6. Ibid., p. 92.

7

The wear-and-tear theory [of aging] states that all cells at their formation are endowed . . . with a definite amount of enzymes and potential energy which during life activities is gradually exhausted in the form of kinetic energy. This quantum energy limits functions and lifespan of every cell. . . . If the exhausted or dead cells or debris are promptly eliminated or liquified by the circulating or the intracellular proteases, or if their level is raised by an enzyme supply given, the progressing aging process may be delayed.[1]
—Max Wolf, M.D., and Karl Ransberger, Ph.D., in *Enzyme Therapy*

Magic Enzymes

There is no way you can fully understand and appreciate your body's amazing ability to heal itself until you come to some kind of grasp of the need for and nature of enzymes.

I have often reflected on the thought that I wish I had known in my younger years more of what I know now as I have advanced into the mid-half-century years. G.B. Shaw is credited with the statement, "Isn't it a shame that youth is wasted on the young!" The idea is, of course, that youth carries with it the energy, vitality, and zest that are so often lacking in the middle and later years.

Cicero thought much on old age. "Old age, especially an honored old age, has so great authority that this is of more value than all the pleasures of youth." In one of his many disputations he reflected: "For as I like a young man in whom there is something of the old, so I like an old man in whom there is something of the young; and he who follows this maxim, in body will possibly be an old man, but he will never be an old man in mind."

The famous German artist and cartoonist Wiihelm Busch (1832-1908) cautioned, ''Youth should heed the older-witted. . . .'' All of this lays the groundwork for this much-needed look at our magic enzymes—their effect on our total well-being from the cradle to the grave.

Appreciating Our Enzyme System

Appreciating our enzyme system is to recognize that life is largely the result of biochemical reactions and that these reactions depend entirely upon the catalyzing effect of enzymes.

What are enzymes? Enzymes are catalysts—the essential biological catalysts that make life possible. We live because our bodies contain thousands of different kinds of enzymes that regulate our life processes. Catalysts cause chemical reactions to take place that otherwise would not occur, whether in plant or animal cells. Catalysts make possible, for example, the production of gasoline, the manufacture of plastic dishes and synthetic fabrics, the unplugging of a clogged-up drain, and the rising of the bread dough.

Enzymes are made of protein (similar to the protein that occurs in the white of an egg), and the biological systems that enzymes participate in are the essential biochemical processes that take place in every living cell. There are two chief characteristics of enzymes: they are extremely reactive (i.e., they will speed up reactions to a much greater extent than ordinary catalysts do) and they have what is called ''high specificity.'' They are choosy about what reactions they will catalyze. The enzyme molecules are extraordinarily complex structures composed of thousands of individual atoms in extremely intricate arrangements. These enzyme molecules are composed of several hundred simpler molecules called amino acids that are joined together in what appears under a microscope to be a long chain.

These amino acids in turn are arranged in a precise order, and the chain itself is twisted and tangled into certain special shapes. It is this very thing—the special shape—that permits the enzyme molecule to exert what I call its magic catalytic properties. Ultramodern research techniques have revealed these things to biochemists through their painstaking efforts.

I am sure this sounds incredibly complex, yet we need to get some kind of foothold in our understanding of our enzyme system in order to appreciate the emphasis on working to keep our cells healthy and our bodies in good shape.

Pushing Back the Curtain of Mystery

As science continues to push back the curtain of mystery that surrounds our living processes, the role that enzymes play in the chemistry of living things places more emphasis on their value and need than ever before.

The application of enzymology (the knowledge of enzyme activity) is a double-edged sword. Its use in medical diagnosis and treatment is basic in metabolic preventive medicine, but the industrial usages have created a technological monster in many instances.

One of the greatest travesties and tragedies in medicine is that we do not utilize the knowledge of enzyme activities in the body, and so instead we attempt to alleviate the condition and treat it as a basic biochemical and metabolic abnormality. Far too often what happens is that the physician prescribes treatment that ends up masking the symptoms. Meanwhile, the patient and physician hope that the body will be able to overcome the disease condition.

Understanding the value of these "sparks of life" can have a profound effect on your present health and the prevention of the killer diseases.

It appears that the beginning and later stages of the development of the chronic degenerative diseases are partially and primarily "alimentary." The antinutritional factors of decomposition, putrefaction, and fermentation of poorly digestive, poor-quality food intake are cumulative. And the body cannot maintain good enzyme activity when the necessary nutrients are lacking.

Men of science have always been at odds with each other in the long struggle to gain an understanding of the human body and the conquest of disease. Controversies and misunderstanding have arisen time after time as one branch of science challenges another. Young scientists with bold new ideas challenge the established opinions of older authorities. The old can learn from the young; the young can learn from the old. It is not easy to have one's cherished professional opinions challenged by members of a new generation. Nevertheless, conflicts like this have opened the doors to tremendous discoveries heralding long-awaited medical advances. Information of incredible intricacy and complexity has unraveled the tangled threads of mystery surrounding the functioning living organisms at the most fundamental levels.

To trace the discovery of enzymes is to uncover names well-known in science and philosophy—Democritus, Plato, Aristotle, Epicurus, Descartes, Paracelsus, Silvius, Lavoisier, de Reaumur, Spallanzani, Beaumont, Schwann, Pasteur, Berzelius, Kühne, Buchner, Liebig, Payen, Persoz, Fischer, Wöhler, Mulder, Willstätter, Sumner, and Northrop.

This brings us to the year 1926, marked in science as the year of the establishment of the protein nature of enzymes. This was the beginning of the modern science of enzymology. What has come about since that time is almost unbelievable. Medicine has learned to use enzymes as diagnostic tools and as therapeutic aids.

In 1978 two Americans and a Swiss won the 1978 Nobel Prize for medicine for their genetic discoveries that could help in prevention and treatment of cancer, diagnose the cause of birth defects, and play a key role in the process of test-tube baby births. The three men—Drs. Daniel Nathans and Hamilton Smith of Johns Hopkins University in Baltimore, Maryland, and Dr. Werner Arber of Basil University, Switzerland, were cited for their "discovery of restriction enzymes and their application to problems of molecular genetics" (The Nashville Banner, October 12, 1978).

David M. Locke in *Enzymes—The Agents of Life* traced the gradual historical recognition that life is largely the result of biochemical reactions and that these reactions occur solely because they are catalyzed by enzymes; he concluded that where we are now in our knowledge of enzymes leaves us looking back at a path littered with controversy and pitted with misunderstanding.

Interestingly enough, many early researchers and philosophers had a view of life that Locke (in his book) and others have called "vitalism"—the idea that focused attention on the unique "vitality" of living things. It was an "instinctive" belief that living creatures in general, and mankind in particular, were activated by inner spirits.

"Mechanism"—another philosophical approach to the nature of the living organism—came into prominence in the seventeenth century through the influence of Descartes, the French philosopher and mathematician. Descartes believed that the behavior of all animals (except mankind, because of his free will) could be accounted for in strictly mechanical terms. But even in man, Descartes believed, the body itself was a mechanical unit capable of maintaining itself without the soul, which largely devoted itself to the processes of higher thought and did not take part in the routine operations of the body. His philosophical speculations caught the temper of his time and became enormously influential.

But the phenomena of life is as old as man's thoughts. Bildad the Shuhite, one of Job's antagonists, said: "Read the history books and see—for we were born but yesterday and know so little; our days here on earth are as transient as shadows. But the wisdom of the past will teach you. The experience of others will speak to you, reminding you that those who forget God have no hope. They are like rushes without any mire to grow in; or grass without water to keep it alive. Suddenly it begins to wither, even before it is cut. A man without God is trusting in a spider's web. Everything he counts on will collapse" (Job 8:8-14 TLB).

It has been estimated that, in all, the body contains a hundred thousand different kinds of enzymes. Each, of course, has its indispensable role to play in maintaining the smooth functioning of the body. Among their functions is the important role of freeing *amino acids* for use by the body.

And what are amino acids? Amino acids are nitrogenous organic compounds that serve as units of structure of the proteins and are essential to human metabolism. We might call them the building blocks from which body tissue is made.

The Process of Digestive Chemical Reactions

Before our foods (both solid and liquid) can be made usable by the human body, they must first become digested, absorbed, or assimilated. Digestion means breaking down our intake into the simplest parts of these foods. We all know what indigestion is. In the case of indigestion, the body has encountered difficulty in digesting what we have taken into our mouth, stomach, and intestines. Somewhere along the line something has contributed to this—the action of enzymes is required to break down our food material. Enzymes must be secreted and present all the way down the digestive tract before the foods can be assimilated and become available for cell utilization.

Enzymes, remember, are catalysts—i.e., they enter into a chemical reaction by speeding up the chemical reaction. Amazingly, the enzyme remains unchanged at the end of the interaction, and it can take part in a new similar reaction. So a small amount of enzyme material can do the same work over and over again.

An enzyme may also initiate a biochemical reaction, it may slow down or inhibit a biochemical reaction, and it may stop the reaction. An enzyme may be likened to a preacher who is necessary for a marriage ceremony, but he does not enter into the marriage bond between the two marrying individuals.

All of the biologic or metabolic processes in the body are initiated and controlled by enzyme activities. Remember also, I told you that enzymes as catalysts are quite selective about what they will or will not do. We do well to pay attention to what our digestive tract is saying to us—it might be trying to tell us that our enzymes are warning us that we are doing something wrong.

When any food material is taken into our mouths, an enzyme called ptylin is mixed with our saliva. Ptylin is an amylase or carbohydrate-splitting enzyme. The action of ptylin is naturally assisted by the degree that we chew and mix our food with the saliva.

When we swallow our food and it passes into the stomach, it is then acted upon by the enzyme, pepsin, and hydrochloric acid. Pepsin splits protein and will work only in an acid medium. If the contents of the mixture in the stomach are not made acid by the hydrochloric secretions, then the pepsin enzyme cannot function. The proteins are broken down into pelypettides. The food is mechanically churned as it is being digested and becomes a food mass known as a bolus.

After varying periods of time, depending on the food material, the little gate at the end of the stomach relaxes and the bolus passes into the small intestine. This is an intestinal tube that is looped in the abdominal cavity and is usually about 20 feet long. This is where the main digestion and absorption occurs. Near the palorous is a small channel or duct coming from the gallbladder known as the bile duct. As the food comes into the small intestine a message goes to the gallbladder and there is an outpouring of bile via this duct. This bile mixes with any fat food, emulsifying it to give the larger fat particles smaller surface areas so the bile salts and bile acids can function more efficiently.

The combination of digestive fluid in the small intestinal tract is called the succus entericus and is quite complex. It is alkaline in reaction and contains three main groups of enzymes. The first enzyme is called lipase, whose function is to break down the emulsified fat into its smaller components, fatty acids, and glycerols. The second is anylaise, which acts on carbohydrates. Trypsin is the third digestive secretion component and works on proteins to reduce them to amino acids.

Enzyme Companions

Do the enzymes get any help? Indeed they do. Certain accessory substances play important roles in helping and hindering enzymes as they go about their business of accelerating the all-important biochemical reactions. These materials are called, appropriately, coenzymes. Among these are the vitamins. Now you begin to understand why vitamins are so essential to the diet!

This all sounds very technical, but complex as it all is, the vitamins make possible the function of the complex enzyme systems that constitute the functional apparatus of living cells. You say you are getting all the vitamins you need from the foods you eat—but what if you aren't? Could that be one of the reasons you have indigestion? Or worse—you may have a disturbed enzyme system that may be contributing to the growth of cancer cells or other diseases.

Our heat-treated, enzyme-deficient diets today are endangering our pancreas and salivary glands. There is more and more acknowledgment by men of science that raw, uncooked food in the diet is indispensable to the highest degree of health. The special virtue of raw food is sometimes ascribed to as its "live" quality. The evidence indicates that the unique value of the raw-food diet resides in its enzyme content.

Sober reflection will reveal to the reader that the vital component of enzymes must be supplied by the food we eat and carried to the pancreas by the bloodstream. When the pancreatic juice is subnormal in enzyme content, this is evidence of an enzyme-deficiency condition of the cells of the whole organism (not just the pancreas).

What we *do* know is that in order for the body to digest

protein it requires a multitude of proteolytic enzymes. It has been proposed that these protein-digesting enzymes (mainly from the pancreas) are in fact part of the body's defense system to keep in check any mutant or overpowering cells which present a threat to the body. When we overindulge in dietary intake of protein, the protelytic enzymes may be directed away from their role as part of the body's defense, and instead concentrate their efforts on digesting the dietary protein in the intestine.

If such a theory is true, it would mean that the body is not completely effective in defending itself against cells which it recognizes as a potential threat. It allows some of those cells to survive because one of its major defense components, the enzymes, are diverted to a different function, that of digesting dietary protein. These cells may then continue dividing, if conditions permit, until a chaotic mass of unorganized autonomous cells results.[2]

Dr. Harold Manner, in setting forth that information in his well-researched book *The Death of Cancer*, stresses that at this juncture in time this is still just a theory. But he emphasizes that when cancer is still such a mystery, one should not discount any theory, however tenuous, until the answer to cancer has been irrefutably solved.

We know that every day over a thousand people fall prey to the devastating affects of cancer. Since this book is primarily directed to the subject of cancer and coronary, the question is in order, "How do the magic enzymes relate to these diseases?"

How Does Cancer Kill?

Cancer kills by robbing the body of nutrients. The cancer cells are no longer a part of the body which exists for the good of the whole, but they become an autonomous, voracious entity in direct competition with the organism for survival. The cancer cells have slipped out of the control mechanisms which could have prevented their survival.

We have talked about amino acids and glucose. We know that amino acids are needed for protein synthesis in normal cells, but they are also used by malignant cells. These robber cancer cells trap nitrogen, and the direction of amino acids then becomes a one-way street—and chaotic growthrate takes place. Glucose, you will recall, is the major fuel source in the body and the basic compound into which many foods are converted. The cancer tumor, for some reason, seems better equipped to capture glucose than normal cells, and it acts as a glucose trap. The cancer cells have this voracious energy, therefore, which they use for unrestrained, uncontrolled growth, that lacks any useful function.

An understanding of enzymes, the role of good nutrition, and a proper lifestyle can get us back on the road to good health. As Dr. Manner emphasizes, "We must use our heads to protect our bodies. We must prevent disease to preserve mankind."[3]

What About Other Diseases?

The enzyme content of the pancreas in a cadaver (a dead body) shows that amylase, lipase, and trypsin are markedly diminished in those individuals dying of diabetes, tuberculosis, and cancer. Liver diseases, colitis and gastric disorders, ulcer and gallbladder disease, diabetus mellitus, and other chronic degenerative diseases are known to be directly related to enzyme activity. Enzymes are of cardinal importance in supporting healthful living. Enzymes emerge as a true yardstick of vitality.

The Aim of Nutrition

A primary aim of nutrition should be to identify individual nutritional requirements and assure the intake and utilization of these essential nutrients.

The "vitalist" thinking of early man is synonymous with what is known today as "enzyme activity," "enzyme value," or "enzyme energy."

Age is not so much a matter of days or years as of the physical condition of the tissues. Functional and structural changes that occur with the aging process can be greatly minimized if we keep our enzyme reserve and activity high. The secretion of digestive enzymes in the stomach, intestinal tract, and pancreas will tend to lessen as we get older and malnourishment takes its toll.

Experiments at such places as Brown University and Carnegie Institution have produced some important conclusions regarding the influence of food upon the lifespan and the speed of metabolism. It was shown that an increase in quantity of food produced a higher rate of metabolism, as evidenced by increase in speed of the heart, and thus the individuals completed the life cycle in a shorter time. The researcher Ingle and his collaborators concluded that length of life is dependent upon a definitely limited sum total of energy which the organism has to expend, and life normally ends when the energy limits have been reached. It follows that, if an organism dissipates its supply of energy quickly, death occurs sooner than if the energy is expended slowly. . . . Failure to recognize the identity and oneness of enzymes and vital energy embarrasses development of a clearer understanding of what constitutes health, disease, and life, and is in the end injurious to an optimal state of health.[4]

The enzyme content of organisms is depleted with increasing old age; and when the enzyme content becomes so low that metabolism cannot proceed at a proper level, death will overtake the organism. Why then do some people live longer? It has become a proven scientific fact that length of life depends on how you digest and use the foods you eat. And food digestion and use depends on enzymes. We have already seen that every living thing must have enzymes to keep alive.

Since there is evidence indicating a reduced secretion of pancreatic enzymes with advancing age, it is important that we recognize as early in life as possible that we must guard wisely this gift of health in order to insure maintenance of enzyme activity throughout our lifetime.

One of the things we can all do to help ourselves is to eat more slowly. Insufficient mastication (and bolting of food) tends to decrease the flow of saliva and places an extra burden on the subsequent digestive processes. If you do that all through life, you will pay the penalty as you advance in age. Therefore, as much as possible, avoid hurried eating. Another thing anyone can do is to avoid flushing food down with liquids. This is not conducive to maximum digestive efficiency. Defective dentures add to the problem, particularly as one gets older.

The reason so many older people tire easily and complain of being tired is because their bodies lack enzymes. The food they eat cannot be utilized constructively but is turned instead into toxins—poisons which lead to sickness. Enzymes are apparently the key to longevity, neutralizing the basic causes of aging and enabling the body to retain its youthful qualities.

Emotional disturbances have their effect on digestive enzymes also. Flatulence, dyspepsia, heartburn, or the feeling of excessive fullness after eating may be the result of enzyme activity caused by worry, fear, or stress.

We hear the statement, "You are as young as your arteries," and that is not to be discounted; but we might also say, "You are as young as your enzymes."

The emphasis on eating as many raw, uncooked foods as possible is of great significance. In the manufacture and cooking of food, enzymes are killed because they cannot stand heat. We cannot, therefore, get the enzymes we all need from outside sources; we must depend on our own bodies to manufacture them. How can you help your body in this task of providing an active enzyme system? You can make certain that your diet contains an adequate supply of protein. Protein, you will recall, provides the essential amino acids that are used to make the body's own enzymes. Whether one is consuming animal or vegetable protein, it must be of good quality if it is to meet the body's demanding requirements.

Then, it is essential to insure an adequate supply of vitamins and minerals so that all the enzyme systems of your body will be in what is called a fully functional state. As we get older, there may be an insufficient blood supply to the digestive tract as a result of atherosclerosis or cardiac insufficiency. This can result in atrophy of the intestinal mucusa. The intestinal wall becomes friable and sensitive, which impedes reabsorption and assimilation of the nutrients from the intestinal tract.

As muscular atrophy of both the large and small intestine occurs, along with the diminished secretion of the protective mucus, we develop more evidence of the effects of poor digestion and assimilation as age advances. Many older people will develop diverticulosis of the large intestine; tissues will usually be symptomatic, and the pockets of diverticuli will become inflamed.

All of this points to one thing—the need to begin a prevention program as early in life as possible in order to ward off the possibility of these things happening.

Superoxide Dismutase (SOD)

SOD is an enzyme. Perhaps now you can better understand why it had such a beneficial effect on my daughter. SOD appears to have its main benefits in preventing the destructive effects of superoxide, the highly reactive free radical in the cell which consists of an oxygen molecule with only one electron. The typical oxygen molecule has two electrons, so the free radicals are molecules (or parts of molecules) with only one electron. The chemical bond that acts as the glue that keeps all of our molecules in our body together consists of pairs of electrons. A free radical with one single electron is unstable.

Someone has likened a free radical to a convention delegate

away from his wife. It is a highly reactive chemical agent that will combine with anything that is around. A free radical has also been likened to a rapist, and to worsen things, a free radical's attack on another molecule can sometimes be so violent that it will create other free radicals, thus setting off a small chain reaction of deterioration in the cell. SOD speeds up the deactivation of the superoxide free radical so that there are less toxic products formed. By decreasing the concentration of the superoxide free radicals, SOD prevents many adverse and destructive oxidation reactions. These injurious oxidation reactions have been tied into the chronic degenerative diseases as well as to accelerated aging.

Professor A.M. Michelson (Institute de Biologie Physio Clinique, France) has studied SOD and found out that when he added carcinogens (cancer-causing agents) and SOD to cell cultures, the SOD protected the cell cultures so that they did not become abnormal. It seemed that the addition of SOD increased the cell's functional quality. SOD is nature's way of detoxifying the deadly superoxide that is so prevalent in our society today.

The Pagans of the Body

The story is told of a doctor who was thoroughly converted. He wrote: "I had been horizontally converted, but not vertically. I had been born of water but not of the Spirit. Now I've been born of the Spirit. Now I'm going to work on the pagans of the body—cancer cells—in a new spirit."

This man was a cancer specialist. Dr. E. Stanley Jones, in telling this, makes the observation, "He was right, for cancer cells are cells turned selfish. They refuse to serve the rest and demand that the rest serve them. Hence the cancer. He [the doctor] said that they represented life—life turned in the wrong direction and hence destroying itself and others. He said that if he could convert these pagan cells to healthy ends, he could save them and the body.

"All life is cancerous if it is turned toward itself and refuses to serve, wanting to be served."

We have seen some of the things that are contributing to the deadly work of these pagans of the body.

The Apostle Paul in speaking of the relationship between husbands and wives makes an analogy that is worth looking at. He says that husbands are to love their wives as [being in a sense] their own bodies. "For no man ever hated his own flesh, but nourishes *and* carefully protects and cherishes it, as Christ does the church" (Eph. 5:29 Amp.).

Judging from the increasing numbers of people who are becoming cancer statistics, one questions whether we are nourishing and carefully protecting and cherishing our bodies as well as we should. The psalmist, in talking about sickness, makes this observation: "Fools because of their transgression, and because of their iniquities, are afflicted" (Ps. 107:17).

FOOTNOTES

1. Max Wolf, M.D., and Karl Ransberger, Ph.D., *Enzyme Therapy* (Los Angeles: Regent House, 1977), p. 114.
2. Dr. Harold W. Manner, *The Death of Cancer* (Evanston, Ill., Advanced Century Publishing Co., 1978), pp. 139, 140.
3. Ibid., p. 147.
4. Edward Howell, *The Status of Food Enzymes in Digestion and Metabolism* (Chicago: National Enzyme Co., 1946), p. 72.

8

Cancer is not a single cellular problem; it is an accumulation of numerous damaging factors combined in deteriorating the whole metabolism, after the liver has been progressively impaired in its function. Therefore, one has to separate two basic components in cancer: a general one and a local one. The general component is mostly a very slow, progressing, imperceptible symptom caused by poisoning of the liver and simultaneously an impairment of the whole intestinal tract, later producing appearances of vitally important consequences all over the body.

—Dr. Max B. Gerson
in *A Cancer Therapy*

Love Your Liver

Your liver is the key—the key to your body's health and its ability to resist disease. Few men of science will disagree. It is the malfunctioning of the liver that is ultimately responsible for the weakening of your body's defenses. Why do some people fall prey to cancer and others do not? The Sloan-Kettering Foundation has just begun to establish the fact that in a truly healthy person there is a cancer immunity, so that even the implantation of living, active cancer cells will quickly be overcome.

Dr. Max B. Gerson, the controversial cancer specialist (much-loved by those who came under his care and whose lives were saved, and much-maligned by those who differed with him in his efforts), was a man far ahead of the times. Gerson knew and published in his book *A Cancer Therapy* that the source of immunity was a healthfully functioning digestive tract, particularly the liver. Gerson's patients were put on a diet directed toward cleansing the liver of accumulated poisons and building its health through a proper selection of nutrients.

What Is the Liver?

The liver is the largest organ in the body, weighing about four pounds. It is located in the upper-right portion of the abdominal cavity immediately under the diaphragm. The liver has so many functions in relation to health that it is easy to understand why no one can survive its removal. From digestion to purification of the bloodstream and adding to the blood various food elements as they are required, there is no nutrient that does not have some importance to the living, functioning liver.

As will be shown, brewer's yeast (a rich source of vitamin B and high-grade protein) is of enormous value in the maintenance of a healthy liver, as are vitamins A and D, in addition to the antioxidant functions of vitamins C and E.

The liver is essential for the metabolism of carbohydrates, proteins, fats, and minerals; it plays a major role in detoxifying poisons and drugs; it manufactures cholesterol; it is concerned with iron storage and the manufacture of the elements essentially necessary for blood clotting; it converts glucose to glycogen and stores glycogen as a source of energy. And one of its primary functions is the destruction of old red-blood cells and conversion of the hemoglobin molecule into *bilirubin*.

The liver produces a yellowish-green or brown fluid of very bitter taste called bile. This is conveyed from the liver by two ducts—the hypotic ducts. These ducts come together to form a common bile duct, which eventually empties into the first part of the small intestine, called the *duodenum*.

The gallbladder, which is a small, pear-shaped sac and serves as a reservoir for concentrated bile, is connected with the bile duct. The main components of bile are bile salts and bile pigments. Since bile is strongly alkaline in reaction, it neutralizes the acid coming into the duodenum from the stomach. Bile salts are reabsorbed and reused. These salts promote efficient digestion of fats by detergent action, which gives very fine emulsification of fatty materials. This not only assists digestion, but also provides (perhaps more importantly) efficient absorption of fat elements by filli of the intestines.

Pollutants and Your Liver

We have already seen how the body is continually assaulted by many pollutants that can cause cancer. Many of these cancer-causing pollutants can be detoxified by enzymes (particularly B-complex vitamins and coenzymes). They cause oxidation reactions, and oxidation reaction is all-important in normal cell health.

Since we hold to the view that cancer is basically cells gone wild, the importance of keeping adequate oxygen in the blood can be seen. Dr. Otto Warburg, who distinguished himself in the fight against cancer, has shown that normal cells use oxygen-based reactions as their source of energy, and that cells not supplied with adequate oxygen must switch to a lower-energy system based on glucose for their survival. And this conversion produces a cancer cell. In other words, normal cells use oxygen, while cancer cells don't. Cancer cells thrive on glucose, but are killed by oxygen. Thus the B-complex vitamins may play a role in preventing a normal cell from switching to a cancer cell by maintaining a proper oxygen-fueled energy system.

What does this have to do with pollution and the liver?

In 1970, Dr. Warburg demonstrated that a vitamin B-1 deficiency would start the cancerous process in cells. He told Nobel Prize winners that a plentiful supply of niacin (B-3), riboflavin (B-2), and pantothenic acid (B-5) is the best possible protection against cancer. And he believed in keeping adequate oxygen in the blood along with daily exercising and vitamins E and B-15[1].

Pangamic acid is the chemical name for vitamin B-15 (found in seeds, liver, yeast, and brain), and this increases the body's efficiency in using oxygen at the cellular level. Pangamic acid helps to protect the liver. And a healthy liver will help keep pollutants in the body at a low level. Pangamic acid also helps keep the liver healthy by preventing fat-infiltration damage when the liver is overly bombarded with pollutants or alcohol.

There isn't too much that we as individuals can do to reverse the environmental pollution which is all around us, but we can in our own bodies promote an environment which will help prevent cancer. We know that carcinogens are considered to be the largest indirect cause of cancer, and they are numbered in the thousands. Cigarette smoke, chemicals, low-level radiation, hair sprays, mothballs, insecticides, food additives, flourides, and even chlorine in our water are suspected or have been proved as causes of cancer. Carcinogens are cellular poisons; as has been pointed out, the cumulative effects of carcinogens will in time destroy or disrupt intracellular machinery and cause cancer. The scientific research confirming this is available for our reading and examination. What this is doing to our livers is causing acute liver failure.

If the liver functions improperly because of poor nutrition, or is damaged by the bombardment of poisons in the diet and in the atmosphere, then it will not be able to detoxify at the rate it should to keep the body in good health. It is time we stop deluding ourselves about our state of health.

Jethro Kloss, lecturer, teacher, and pioneer developer of natural health and healing methods, tells of working in the emergency room of a hospital just to gain valuable experience. He witnessed scores of postmortems under competent surgeons. "It was very interesting to see the organs of people whose lives we had previously known, and knew just what they had been in the habit of eating and drinking.

"We opened up one man who had been a great eater of

meats, rich pastries, pies, cakes, puddings, white bread, peel-
ed potatoes, etc. We found his liver about three times its normal size. There were tumors all around the liver, and some in
the liver, ranging in size from a small marble to a small-sized
potato. The heart was also very much enlarged, more than
once again its normal size, and the walls of the heart were
very thick and flabby and of a dark color, as if bloodshot. The
spleen and pancreas were both enlarged and diseased, and he
had gallstones and gravel in the bladder. His stomach was
also very much prolapsed and diseased.

"He was a middle-aged man, quite fleshy. . . ."[2] That
description fits many middle-aged men and women today!

Most cancer victims have a deficient liver function, and few
will respond to any kind of treatment unless this is dealt with.
Actually, more people are dying from toxicity than of the
disease itself.

Eydie Mae Hunsberger is a recovered cancer patient who
believes strongly in what she calls ''the living foods diet'' and
the use of wheatgrass. Wheatgrass contains abscisic acid,
which reverses the growth of cancerous tumors. Eydie Mae
chose the unconventional way to fight cancer in her body. She
went to Ann Wigmore and the Hippocrates Health Institute
in Boston. Eydie's story is told in her book *How I Conquered
Cancer Naturally.*[3]

Detoxification of the whole body and then going on the
''living foods'' diet (fruit and vegetable combinations that
complement each other) were the tools Eydie Mae and her
husband used in their fight against death. Eydie Mae is alive
and healthy today. Her cancer was discovered in 1973.

Jacqueline Verrett and Jean Carper in their controversial
book *Eating May Be Hazardous to Your Health* point out that
all of us are involved in a gigantic experiment of which we
may never know the outcome, at least in our lifetime.
Possibly our children and grandchildren will be able to look
at what has been written and recall what has been said, and
they will say, ''They were right!'' One wishes this were not

the case, but every indication leads us to suspect that this will happen. Just how dangerous, just how hazardous are the foods we eat? Are they contributing to cancer? To birth defects? To mutations? To liver, brain, and heart damage, and to a hundred other diseases? There can be only one answer—prevent it. Know the facts, then return to what the safest authority of all—the Word of God—has to say, and live according to the Good Book.

Nutritional Treatment and B Vitamins

One of the top agencies involved in cancer research is the National Cancer Institute. Dr. H.F. Kraybill, Ph.D., of this institute, published a paper which marshals considerable evidence that nutritional treatment is of value both preventively and therapeutically. While Dr. Kraybill does not refer to Dr. Gerson, what he is saying sounds remarkably similar to what Dr. Gerson advocated.

In his impressive paper, Dr. Kraybill lists these discoveries as being of tremendous importance to cancer research:

> Yeast is particularly effective [for the prevention of liver cancer] since the level of 15 percent of it is almost completely protective, and any high-quality protein diet and B vitamins, especially B_2, are defensive mechanisms in inhibiting formation of such neoplasms.

The doctor points to Japanese and American investigators on liver neoplasia in which riboflavin-rich diets inhibited tumor formation. "In general, the injury of liver cells resulting from a nutrient deficiency may impair normal growth of cells, and carcinogens may then readily induce hepatomatous nodules."[4]

The nutrients pointed out by Dr. Kraybill as having a cancer-preventive effect are all foods that are directly concerned with the health of the liver. Thiamin, riboflavin, and choline are all used principally in the liver, both for digestive functions and for detoxification of the blood. When they are deficient, not only can the liver not function properly, but it also deteriorates.

Dr. Kraybill also incriminated additives in his research findings:

> A consideration of food intake in carcinogenesis is not restricted to nutrition per se but must also include additives, contaminants, or processing degradation products, which may play a more important role in tumor induction.[5]

He then goes down the list from heated or processed fats to spices, plastics, petroleum by-products, and food colors and flavor additives as established or probable causes of cancer. These are all materials known to have toxic effects on the liver and may quite conceivably gradually diminish the body's resistance to cancer.

What About Liver for the Liver?

Love your liver; keep it in good health. To do so is to greatly improve your chances of being able to resist and overcome any incipient cancer.

Nutritionists, scientists, men of medicine—almost anywhere you turn in books on the subject—everyone and everything points to the fact that the very best food for liver health is liver itself.

"Why does it have to taste so awful?" There are those who howl and ask that question. Liver is best taken when it has not been altered by cooking; therefore, your best bet is desiccated liver—one of the most valuable food supplements that can be included in anybody's diet.

Adelle Davis, America's celebrated nutritionist whose early books *Let's Get Well* and *Let's Eat Right to Keep Fit* first alerted many an individual to the importance of proper diet and the use of supplements, was a strong advocate of eating liver and using it in various ways in one's diet.

> When I am working under pressure, I eat liver daily for breakfast, searing it lightly on both sides with a little vegetable oil, then letting it cook slowly, uncovered. Both raw and rare liver are nutritionally superior to well-done. Every type of liver, however . . . supplies excellent protein, iron,

copper, trace minerals, and all the B vitamins, including those especially needed during stress.

If you are one of those people who hate liver yet truly desire the best health you can obtain, desiccated liver, dried under vacuum below body temperature, is available; not by the farthest stretch of the imagination, however, could one call it palatable; 2 heaping teaspoons are equivalent to one serving, or ¼ pound, of fresh liver. . . . I have been surprised at the number of people who not only take it daily but claim it makes them feel so much better that nothing could make them give it up. I use it, stirred into water or tomato juice, when I cannot get fresh liver. Tablets of dried liver are expensive; 30 tablets are usually equivalent to a serving, or ¼ pound, of fresh liver.[6]

A friend who was suffering from extreme fatigue, for whom Adelle suggested liver daily for breakfast for a time, did his best but sent her this complaint:

My dear Adelle, it is plain_____to follow your directions;
But I do try hard, avoid all lard and all the fine confections.

There is much to encourage and much to intrigue,
So much to be grateful for this lack of fatigue.

When devotion to you and in spite of my pride . . .
One thing that I can hardly abide

Is rising each morning at the clang of clocks
and facing the white vastness of the icebox
I withdraw with fright and begin to shiver
on seeing that mountain of slippery liver.

But once it is down, I lift high my cup,
And I can drink deep of the milk and pep-up.[7]

The incidence of liver cancer is especially high in Japan, Korea, and other Oriental countries. The reason for this, most researchers agree, is that the Oriental diet consists largely of polished rice, which is deficient in the B-complex vitamins, particularly riboflavin. The Sloan-Kettering Foundation has done some important experiments relative to cancer of the liver, using rats. They were able to produce liver cancer by using polished rice and Butter Yellow in their diets. Dividing the rats into control groups and feeding them 15 percent brewer's yeast produced rats without liver cancer.

Milligram for milligram, brewer's yeast is the richest known source of the B vitamins (so important in maintenance of a healthy, functioning liver), followed closely by desiccated liver. (Brewer's yeast can be bought as a food supplement in both powder and tablet form.)

How Can One Get Enough B Vitamins?

Nature has arranged it so that, in their natural states, cereals and also protein foods supply B vitamins. The problem arises, however, when we used processed and refined grains and cereals from which these valuable B-vitamin properties have been destroyed by heat. And much is lost through the cooking and preparation of protein food sources. Many nutritionists and doctors tell us that our "balanced diets" provide all of our nutritional requirements. But the fact remains that *this just isn't so anymore.* I've already pointed to brewer's yeast and liver, and we can also turn to B-vitamin preparations.

The Balance Wheel of the Body

The liver is the site of many important enzyme and enzomatic and biochemical reactions, and has been compared to a chemical factory and the balance wheel of the body.

Unfortunately, the incidence of liver damage in this country, including often-fatal cirrhosis, is increasing rapidly, even among children. It is not unreasonable to state that probably everyone has liver injury to some extent. Given the circumstances of our environment—our polluted world and the foods we eat—few of us could escape liver damage. There was a time when cirrhosis was confined to chronic alcoholics, but while they suffer much from this disease, it is no longer limited to them. There are some physicians today who consider that the rising rate of liver damage among even the very young can be traced to the appalling consumption of soft drinks. It is not at all unusual to go into an office complex and see at *any* hour of the day vast numbers of the people sipping some type of soft drink.

When this important balance wheel of the body is out of kilter, how will a person know? Slight liver injury causes vague symptoms such as digestive disturbances, loss of energy, and inability to detoxify harmful substances. Sometimes there will be a swelling of the ''stomach'' region. Often the victim will complain of an overall general feeling of illness.

Hepatitis, which is a more severe manifestation of liver inflammation, is usually accompanied by jaundice. This refers to a yellowing of the skin caused by an excess of bile pigments in the circulatory system and in all the tissues of the body. Hepatitis can be caused by viral or bacterial infections, or by exposure to toxic substances including drugs, chemicals, and pesticides.

Cirrhosis of the liver can develop from severe hepatitis. Symptoms may be slight at first, but as the condition progresses, weight loss, nausea, vomiting, complaints of indigestion, and inability to tolerate fats usually occur. There will be noticeable swelling of the legs (edema), and other complications may result, such as enlarged veins in the esophagus.

When it is felt that foods are inefficiently utilized or hormones appear to be excessive in one's body, liver damage should be considered as a possible cause and the diet should be improved accordingly.[8]

An unhealthy liver may produce only half the normal amount of bile needed—enzymes and coenzymes are so reduced that the utilization of all foodstuffs is interfered with —causing chronic indigestion to result.

Can the Liver Regenerate Itself?

The liver does have an amazing capacity to regenerate itself if all essential nutrients are supplied. Diets high in complete proteins, vitamin C, the B vitamins (particularly choline), inisotol, methonine, and especially vitamin E hasten its regeneration.[9] Lecithin is a valuable source of choline, and improvement in one's liver functions are greatly aided by the addition of this valuable nutrient to the diet.

An irreparable stage is reached in liver function if steps are not taken promptly and the situation is allowed to degenerate. Massive scarring can occur in liver damage, but vitamin E, if generously supplied, can speed the healing process and do much to prevent scarring. Scarring can impair circulation, and hemorrhaging is a frequent cause of death in liver-damaged patients.

It is safe to say that of all of the organs of the body, the need to maintain the health of one's liver ranks at the top of the list.

I am fond of telling my patients that we need to start the Inner Order of Liver Lovers so that we will learn to love our livers, so we will have a good liver, and be a long liver, and also so we will be a great lover, because it takes a good liver to be a great lover.

FOOTNOTES

1. Dr. Richard A. Passwater, *Cancer and Its Nutritional Therapies* (New Canaan, Con.: Keats Publishing Co., 1978), p. 151.
2. Jethro Kloss, *Back to Eden* (Santa Barbara: Lifeline Books, 1972), p. 23.
3. Eydie Mae with Chris Loeffler, *How I Conquered Cancer Naturally* (Irvine, Calif.: Harvest House Publishers, 1975).
4. J.I. Rodale & Staff, *Cancer Facts and Fallacies* (Emmaus, Penna.: Rodale Books, Inc., 1969), p. 229.
5. Ibid., p. 230.
6. Adelle Davis, *Let's Eat Right to Keep Fit* (New York: Signet Books, Harcourt Brace Jovanovich, 1970), pp. 104-5.
7. Ibid., p. 108.
8. Adelle Davis, *Let's Get Well* (New York: Signet Books, New American Library, 1972), p. 172.
9. Ibid.

> Many are victims of fear and worry because they fail properly to maintain their spiritual nutrition. . . .
>
> The majority of people liberally feed their bodies, and many make generous provision for their mental nourishment; but the vast majority leave the soul to starve, paying very little attention to their spiritual nutrition; and as a result the spiritual nature is so weakened that it is unable to exercise the restraining influence over the mind which would enable it to surmount its difficulties and maintain an atmosphere above conflict and despondency.
>
> —Dr. William Sadler
> in *Practice of Psychiatry*

Freedom from Fear

Fear is an emotion that everyone experiences in some form or another from time to time. What we fear may vary from person to person, but the crippling, devastating results of fear can play havoc with one's health and total well-being. Those of us in the medical profession know only too well what fear can do to an individual.

The fear of developing cancer is a specter that haunts many people. All segments of our population fall prey to this fear. Few, it appears, are immune, although many individuals have learned how to handle their fears.

Why this widespread fear? One reason may be because cancer-associated health organizations have done an effective job in alerting the populace to the seven danger signals associated with cancer. These early-detection campaigns are necessary.

Scarcely a family is exempt from the heartache that accompanies the news that a family member has developed cancer. Fear grips the heart and catches at one's throat. The mind goes into a numbed state of shock. If family members are not cancer victims, we know friends, business acquaintances, or neighbors—someone who has been confronted with the grim news that cancer has invaded the body.

Death is a robber. And although a cancer victim may go into a state of remission or be pronounced "cured," or be told that the prescribed treatment has been effective, fear still lurks in the back of his mind and the minds of those who know and love him. It is the fear that one day the cancer will again rear its ugly head and eventually be the thing that sends him to his grave. To be plagued by anxious fear is very real and painful. Tolstoy, writing in *War and Peace,* declared, "Man can be master of nothing while he fears death, but he who does not fear it possesses all."

Fear has many forms. There is even the kind of fear that can be a friend rather than a foe. This is the kind of instinctive emotion that signals impending danger and helps us make right reactions. Then there are the exaggerated and irrational fears which sometimes have their roots in childhood experiences, or have been caused by emotional conflicts, buried memories, or other factors.

As it relates to the fear of developing cancer or facing the reality of cancer in a loved one, among other things we fear what the cancer will cost. And that is a very valid concern. Almost everyone has read or heard accounts of families who have been devastated financially by the health-care costs incurred in treating a loved one. Prolonged hospitalization, a lingering disease, radiation and chemotherapy treatments— all this has been known to wipe out a family.

Many people mistakenly think that the major-medical clause in their health insurance policy will automatically pay for everything, including prolonged hospitalization and treatment for cancer. According to *Parade* magazine

(February 4, 1979) in a news story entitled "Facing the Unthinkable," "Estimates have it that only 30 to 60 percent of actual medical treatment costs for cancer are reimbursed, and many forms of cancer are extremely expensive. A recent study by Cancer Care Inc. reports overall cancer expenses in the $5,000 to $50,000 range, with a median of $19,000 spent over two years."

There are thousands of American families who have opted for specific disease insurance to cover the gap between general-health-plan benefits and other costs. Cancer insurance is a hotly debated subject in and around insurance circles, but it is alleviating some of the fear formerly held, particularly by those whose family history suggests a susceptibility to the disease.

If one steps outside the bounds of accepted orthodox practice, there is the concern about what others will think. We fear the criticism of others. We wonder, too, if the insurance companies would honor nonorthodox treatment claims. We fear what our doctor will think if we opt for an approach that is different. Many things spark fear.

A friend relates that her daughter called one evening and inquired, "Mother, do you believe in James 5:14 and 15?" She was momentarily caught off-guard but then quickly responded, "I believe in the whole Bible." As she replied, she reached for her Bible. Quickly turning the pages, she read, "Is any sick among you? Let him call for the elders of the church; and let them pray over him, anointing him with oil in the name of the Lord: And the prayer of faith shall save the sick, and the Lord shall raise him up. . . ."

Her daughter continued, "Mother, I've been told by my doctor that I have a large growth on my female organs and that I've got to have an immediate operation. If I have the operation it means I'll never be able to have children. I know there is always the possibility that the growth might be malignant. . . ." There was a pause. As she paused, her mother felt caught up in fear.

"Mom, I believe those verses too, but I had to hear it from you as well. I'm going to ask the elders of the church to do just as the Bible instructs. I believe God wants me healthy and He wants me to have children."

My friend felt the fear vanish as her daughter confidently voiced her belief that God wanted her well. It was an unorthodox approach, an approach not practiced nearly as much by Christians today as it should be. The elders of that particular church had never anointed anyone with oil or followed that biblical injunction. But they honored this young woman's request.

A year later the mother had occasion to be in a home prayer meeting where she met the elder who did the actual anointing with oil. "Even as we laid hands on her and did this, we sensed that God was honoring this prayer of faith, both on the part of your daughter, and because we as elders were free of fear but had bold confidence and faith as well."

Today that young woman is the mother of a beautiful and healthy son. Indeed, the operation never took place. The very next day the doctor declared that the growth had "mysteriously disappeared."

Faith Can Replace Fear

Fear can translate itself into bodily illness. The annals of medical history are full of such cases. Dr. S.I. McMillen wrote an eye-opening book in 1963 that set the Christian bookselling world on the alert. Nothing quite like this had reached their hands before. The secular book-selling world took note also. The book *None of These Diseases* became a best-seller. The author, a modest, unassuming medical doctor, wrote in his Preface:

> Peace does not come in capsules! This is regrettable because medical science recognizes that emotions such as fear, sorrow, envy, resentment, and hatred are responsible for the majority of our sicknesses. Estimates vary from 60 percent to nearly 100 percent.

> Emotional stress can cause high blood pressure, toxic goiter, migraine headaches, arthritis, apoplexy, heart trouble, gastrointestinal ulcers, and other serious diseases too numerous to mention. As physicians we can prescribe medicine for the symptoms of these diseases, but we cannot do much for the underlying cause—emotional turmoil. *It is lamentable that peace does not come in capsules.*
>
> We need something more than a pill for the disease-producing stresses. . . .
>
> This book was born as a result of a thousand sighs for the many people who left my office without receiving adequate help. . . .[1]

Dr. McMillen related that there wasn't time to do much more than prescribe some pills for people's complaints, but he knew there was something more, something better than pills for them to take for the rest of their lives. I fully understand what he was saying.

What is that something more, that something better?

Faith *can* replace fear. And we have a faith-honoring God. This is not to guarantee that God always honors that faith with a miraculous healing, for that is not the case. Nor is this book trying to answer the question, "Why not?" But it is to acknowledge that God exists and is very real and is a very present help in time of trouble and at *all* times.

Disease Is Not the Perfect Will of God

What about disease and God? Why disease? Why ill-health? Does the Christian faith have anything to do with the body, or is it only concerned with the saving of the soul and getting a person ready for eternity?

God has given us the Bible as His written Word to communicate eternal truth to us. No one understands the human frame better than the One who created it. The Bible has much to say about the proper care and nurture of the body. That is just one part of the Word of God, however, and is not its major teaching.

Christianity is not a healing cult, although many pseudoreligions and cults have made it out to be that very thing. The primary purpose of Christianity is not to keep our bodies in repair. There are those who turn to God only as a last resort, a sort of emergency fire escape using God as some sort of cosmic convenience.

The Christian faith is not a success cult or a happiness-only cult either. One should never lose sight of the indisputable fact that the central purpose of the Christian faith is to redeem man primarily from sin and evil. A by-product of that—called redemption—is a kind of peace and happiness unknown to those outside the Christian faith. Another by-product of that may be true physical healing as God moves in answer to prayer. But to seek health first for health's sake only is to miss the point and to miss God's best.

Contrary to what many think, faith is not some kind of spiritual anesthetic. The peace God offers and to which Dr. McMillen was referring comes in that sweet, unexplainable way as we turn ourselves over to Him, believing in the reality that He is and that He cares. The Bible tells us that God's thoughts are not our thoughts, nor are His ways our ways. If we had our way, no one would die (talk about an over-populated earth!), and no one would suffer.

Disease Was Not God's Idea

God is not to be blamed for human misery; we have inherited what is called the Adamic nature from our first parents, Adam and Eve. Disease was not God's idea. Disease is not the perfect will of God. God wills health, but our sinfulness and our willfulness have brought us to the present state of affairs in the world. To take God at His word, as revealed in His Word, the Bible, and to cooperate with Him, is to experience growth both physically and spiritually—a wholeness that comes in no other way.

God has made a universe of moral and material law; when we break the laws, we break ourselves upon the laws. We will reap the consequences in ourselves. How true it is that some people go through life getting *results,* while others get *consequences.*

Jesus healed people while He ministered here on earth. This was a part of His redemptive impact upon the world, but He asked people to keep quiet about what He had done. This was not His main reason for being. He was first of all a Redeemer from sin and evil, and then a healer of diseases. Jesus insisted on first things first, and that is what we need to heed as well. But He did reach out to the sick and diseased, and He is still reaching out with healing and help today.

Our bodies are a God-given part of us meant to serve us in a mortal world. These bodies are going to wear out, and eventually each of us will die physically. But then it will be replaced by an immortal body, not subject to disease, pain, and decay. The Apostle Paul stared death in the face and exultingly exclaimed, "So when this corruptible shall have put on incorruption, and this mortal shall have put on immortality, then shall be brought to pass the saying that is written, Death is swallowed up in victory. O death, where is thy sting? O grave, where is thy victory? . . . But thanks be to God, which giveth us the victory through our Lord Jesus Christ" (I Cor. 15:54, 55, 57).

Someone may well ask, "Is healing only for Christians?" We look at the biblical record. There we see Jesus healing people whether they followed Him or not. It is interesting to note, however, that after they experienced these miraculous healings, they looked upon Jesus in a new way (cf. Luke 4: 36-41; 6:17-19; 8:26-56; and elsewhere throughout the Gospel record).

Is There an Antidote to Fear?

Dr. Francis A. Schaeffer, a much-respected theologian and the founder and director of L'Abri Fellowship in the Swiss Alps, has written many books. One is entitled *He is There and He Is Not Silent,* and another is entitled *The God Who Is There.* Dr. Schaeffer has in past months had ample opportunity to put his faith to the test as he lay in the Mayo Clinic in Rochester, Minnesota, suffering with cancer. His wife, Edith, has authored a compassionate book entitled *Affliction* in which she examines the reality of pain and suffering in our lives—yes, even in the life of someone as dedicated to the Lord's work as her husband.

What these titles indicate, and what these and other authors and books are saying, is that there is a personal God who has shown Himself to be in the form of the Man Jesus. This Man identified with humanity and became one of us. The biblical record is to be accepted. This giant leap of faith is the antidote to fear and despair. But it is much more. It is also the door that assures us of access to eternal life. Death no longer is to be feared. Our last enemy can be conquered. Death is an enemy, and it is something which God hates, too. Edith Schaeffer explains it like this:

> Death is a part of the battle between Satan and God—and the final victory will be God's. Death will be swallowed up in the victory—the victory of God over Satan and of God's solution to Satan's destructive attack.[2]

As Christians we believe that in the moment of death, when disease has finally taken its toll, the spirit of man leaves the body to go somewhere else:

> We are of good courage, I say, and prefer rather to be absent from the body and to be at home with the Lord.
> —2 Corinthians 5:8 NASB

The peace that does not come in capsules can be found in such places in the Bible as Isaiah 26:3

> Thou wilt keep him in perfect peace, whose mind is stayed on Thee, because he trusteth in Thee.

The peace that cannot be written on a prescription pad and filled at the local drugstore counter comes without cost to us like this:

> Therefore being justified by faith, we have peace with God through our Lord Jesus Christ,

By whom also we have access by faith into this grace wherein we stand, and rejoice in hope of the glory of God.
—Romans 5:1,2

You Ask "Why?"

A college professor and his wife combined their yearly vacation with visiting mission stations in other countries. Since he was also a theologian, he offered his services to the various mission fields from year to year as a visiting minister to the missionaries.

While in the beautiful principality of Monaco in the summer of 1979, serving the Trans World Radio missionaries, the professor began to limp. It was an unaccountable, sudden limping. One beautiful Sunday he was ministering to the needs of others, and the next thing he and his wife knew, the limp had become more obvious. Friends urged him to seek medical advice.

The doctor advised that he return to the states immediately and seek medical help in his own country. A hasty return, by now a noticeable lameness in his right side and arm, and the medical diagnosis is not good. Fear wells up. Yes, even for a godly man.

But for this man and his wife the fear was quickly overcome as quiet trust sprang from the deep levels of their inner being. For years they had been singing hymns about trusting, reading the Word of God, meditating upon it, and preaching and teaching from it. They lived by the precepts they found in the Bible. Now they could stand the test. Isaiah 26:3 became living reality, as did Isaiah 12:2

> Behold, God is my salvation; I will trust and not be afraid, for the Lord Jehovah is my strength and my song; He also has become my salvation.

So long as we are mortal, we shall be confronted with these very natural and human impulses, regardless of our religious convictions or our recognized stature and ability to stand up under pressure. When the possibility of malignancy stares us in the face, it is natural to recoil in fear. It may be only momentary or of short duration, or it may prove to be longer than we might wish or think could happen to us, but terror can roar through one's being. The dread of suffering and pain, the mere thought of death is real. But for the Christian, that one who has entrusted his living *and* his dying to the Lord, the fear and apprehension will not remain.

The college professor immediately underwent brain surgery. There was not one but two tumors. One was removed and it was malignant. Chemotherapy was begun as soon as the wound healed. His future is in God's hands.

The wife of this brave, trusting man could say in agreement with the Apostle:

> For to us has been given the privilege not only of trusting Him
> but also of suffering for Him
> —Philippians 1:29 TLB

But you ask "Why?"

"Why this man? Why Dr. Schaeffer? Why my mother (father, brother, son . . .)? Why?"

If we could understand the "Why?" then we would have the mind of the infinite God. God didn't give the Old Testament Job an answer to his questioning "Why?" There is no detailed explanation. God is sovereign and all-powerful. Our place is to let Him be God while we stay in our place as finite human beings. Edith Schaeffer might have asked "Why?" when confronted with her husband's cancer. Her answer provides insights:

> As we go to the Word of God, we ask for a measure of balance (*a measure,* since none of us can ever have perfect balance —any more than we can be perfect in any other area of life, until Jesus returns). We must look at the whole problem of affliction and suffering which includes death—death of a precious body, death of cells which govern parts of the body, death of personal energy, death of a relationship, death of a state or country. We must talk not in trite phrases, but try to search sufficiently in the blend of facts and examples which the Lord has given to help us. It is important never to feel as if

we were only talking about someone else's problem of sorrow or affliction without facing the reality ourselves. We must let the Word of God speak not only *through* us, but *to* us.[3]

The Age of Anxiety

We are living in what the poet W.H. Auden appropriately called "The age of anxiety." Who would deny it! Defeatist thoughts, with which so many are plagued, trigger fear, and fear goes hand in hand with anxiety. Fear of the unknown makes us anxious. This in turn brings about stress. Stress sets the stage for a host of diseases when the body is not in good metabolic balance. Not the least of these diseases are cancer and coronaries.

Psalm 34:4 tells us what to do: "I sought the Lord, and He heard me, and delivered me from all my fears."

Preventive medicine does not wait passively for symptoms to appear, but works at maintaining body-chemistry balance and rebalancing it whenever it becomes suboptimal. In a biochemically well-balanced body, it is difficult for the cancer process to gain a foothold.

A healthy body is kept in metabolic balance by four main factors:

1. Healthy nutrition and digestion.
2. Healthy elimination.
3. Healthy physical activity.
4. Healthy mental attitude.

We have already seen how it can be thrown out of balance by poisons in the environment or generated within the body by bad habits—too much food, too little food, junk food, badly digested food, alcohol, tobacco, drugs, sedentary habits, irregular sleep, and emotional stress and anxiety.

Preventive medicine places more responsibility on the person who wants to be healthy. It involves a healthy lifestyle for the whole person. For this reason, it is frequently called wholistic (or holistic) health care. We cannot, therefore, ignore the effects of stress.

Right emotions, right thoughts, and right attitudes produce right effects in the body. An outstanding surgeon once told Dr. E. Stanley Jones, "I've discovered the Kingdom of God at the end of my scalpel—it's in the tissues. For the right thing morally is always the healthy thing physically."

William James is credited with saying, "The greatest revolution in my generation was the discovery that human beings by changing their inner attitudes of mind can alter the outer aspects of their lives." That means, of course, for good or ill!

Have you ever considered the wisdom of the proverb which states "For as he thinketh in his heart, so is he" (Proverbs 23:7)?

Emotional stress causes or aggravates disorders of the digestive system, the circulatory system, the genito-urinary system, the nervous system, and the glands of internal secretion, as well as causing allergic disorders, muscle-joint disorders, infections, and eye and skin disease. Dr. McMillen points out, "It's not what you eat—it's what eats you," as he speaks of the effects of emotions on physical health.

God has an answer for this. He condemns such things as sexual immorality (which can produce guilt), hatred, quarreling, jealousy, bad temper, rivalry, factions, party-spirit, envy, drunkenness, and orgies (Galatians 5:19-21).

God calls these "works of the flesh," or sins of the lower nature. Dr. William Sadler (*Practice of Psychiatry*) has stated that the teachings of Jesus if applied to our civilization—and he emphasizes *applied*—would so purify, uplift, and vitalize us that the world would immediately see a new order of human beings possessing superior mental power and increased moral force.

A bitter spirit and the harboring of resentment and hatred can send an individual to an early grave. These are disease-producing emotions, and every doctor in the country sees them at work in his patients daily. There are no medications that can be dispensed to deal with the acids that are produced by an unforgiving spirit in a man or woman.

In the book of Hebrews, the writer speaks of "a bitter spirit" springing up which can poison not only one's own life, but the lives of many others.

A concentration of our energies on ways in which we can make our minds and emotions contribute to health instead of contributing to disease is in order. The British Medical Association states that "there is not a single cell of the body totally removed from the influence of mind and emotions." The American Medical Association states that about 50 percent of diseases are rooted in the physical and an equal percentage rooted in the mental and spiritual faculties.

Most medical doctors would enlarge those percentages to say that more people are passing on the sicknesses of their minds and emotions—their fears and anxieties—to their bodies. One Mayo Clinic doctor said, "We can deal with 25 percent of the people who come to our clinic with our instruments of science, but 75 percent we don't know what to do with. They are passing on the sicknesses of mind and emotion to their bodies, and you can't touch that with the instruments of science."

We know that strong negative emotions such as grief, hate, fear, and anxiety when they do not find an outlet will upset the glandular system and there can be serious after-effects. Many men of science agree that in cancer we see a general breakdown of the whole body, caused by toxins, negative emotions, and improper nutrition. These things together or separately cause hormonal and chemical imbalances resulting in an altered metabolism that is favorable to cancer growth.

To be well is to root out that which upsets our systems. This will require a realistic facing up to the circumstances of our life. Ask yourself some questions: What am I doing that is causing functional disturbance in my system? Am I using this feeling of being unwell as a crutch to gain attention? Do I really want to be well?

To honestly analyze one's emotions and then to take the necessary steps to put an end to the stress of strained relationships and whatever is out of harmony is to gain a foothold in the door of a return to health. Daily we ring up on the register of our emotional makeup our response to the stresses of life. To respond with hatred and resentment and unforgiving attitudes is to invite illness. The body can become predisposed to illness.

Stressful struggle as we reach upward for achievement-oriented success has led many an individual down the road to a heart attack. Coronaries thrive on the pressures exerted upon men and women in the work world. We generally work our way into stressful living as we strive to become someone and make a place for ourselves in our particular corner of the world.

Psychic stress produces adrenaline, and adrenaline calls forth from the fatty deposits of the body the slow but sure killer—cholesterol *(Medical News,* June 2, 1961). Chemicals released in the body as a result of stress produce lethal effects. Diseases from fear are increasing. Not only on the personal level are we confronted with that which raises the blood pressure, but we would have to agree that former President John F. Kennedy was correct when he said that we live under "a nuclear sword of Damocles, hanging by the slenderest of threads, capable of being cut at any moment by accident, miscalculation, or madness."

Not to Become, But to Be

Learn before it is too late that what really counts is not so much what you become in life, but to be God's man or God's woman right where you are. The Apostle Peter was a giant of a man, in my estimation. He was so very human, so like us in his weaknesses and frailties. At one point he calmly said, "Trust yourself to the God who made you, for he will never fail you" (1 Peter 4:19 TLB).

When he advised readers of his letters to give God all their worries and cares, Peter knew what he was talking about (1 Peter 5:7).

God's answer to coronary and cancer and stress-induced

diseases is a conscious and therefore a deliberate effort on our part to involve Him in our decision-making processes. It is a telegram prayer, as it were, to Him: "Lord, how do I handle this?"

There are some people reading these words whom I would imagine have never given the Bible more than a second glance. They scoff at those who uphold it, yet they have never even given it an honest appraisal. "Lord" is a word reserved for expressing one's self forcibly. Recognition of Him as a Person interested in our personal welfare comes slow to many, and to some it never comes because they are God-deniers. Such as these go through life deprived—deprived of power and a strength that could infuse their entire being with a new force.

A look at the word *disease* is interesting. *Dis* is a prefix denoting *separation, negation,* or *reversal.* Affix *dis* to the word *ease* (meaning freedom from pain, worry, or trouble), and you quickly see *dis-ease* as a departure from health, a deviation of the body from that which is normal and healthy.

And that's where we are today as individuals and as a nation. Don Osgood *(Pressure Points: The Christian's Response to Stress)* says "The dis-ease of stressful living is 'piled-up living.' It is a life of carry-over from yesterday's unresolved relationships and circumstances."

Dr. Adler, that famous psychiatrist, put his finger on the problem when he wrote, "It is always the want of social feeling, whatever be the name one gives it . . . living in fellowship, cooperation with humanity . . . which causes an insufficient preparation for all the problems of life. . . . I suppose all the ills of human personality can be traced back to one thing, namely, not understanding the meaning of the statement: 'It is more blessed to give than to receive.' " He is, of course, quoting from the Bible.

Our lovelessness is destructive. It is a form of self-preoccupation producing sickness and dis-ease. Jesus talked about this in the simplest of terms: "Love one another. . . ."

As we search for God's answer to coronary and cancer, we must always come back to what He says in the written Word.

We cannot escape from stress, but we can learn how to live with it, and right relationships are the key. The right vertical relationship, first of all, is with God through Christ. Then the outworking of this comes as we consciously rely upon His help and power and upon the Holy Spirit in our horizontal relationships with others. Ths is not idealistic and unrealistic. It is what the writer of Proverbs called staying on the right path: "Follow the steps of the godly . . . and stay on the right path, for only good men enjoy life to the full" (Proverbs 2:20,21 TLB).

> In all your ways acknowledge Him, and He will direct your paths.
> Be not wise in your own eyes; fear the Lord, and depart from evil.
> It will be health to your navel, and marrow to your bones.
> —Proverbs 3:5-8

The meaning of this is "health to your nerves and sinews, and marrow and moistening to your bones" *(The Amplified Bible)*.

Freedom from fear is possible. The Apostle Paul in his "swan song" letter, the last one he wrote, has given us the answer:

> For God has not given us the spirit of fear, but of power, and of love, and of a sound mind.
> —2 Timothy 1:7

Anxious fear has been known to vanish when individuals have turned their attention and efforts to helping someone else. The Bible records that Job, who suffered much, received God's help in an unusual way: "The Lord turned the captivity of Job when he prayed for his friends" (Job 42:10). Job's captivity was that of being filled with anxious fear.

Freedom from fear can come to the cancer or coronary victim, and to family members and friends. The writer of the Psalms, when praying for deliverance, said, "Give us help from trouble, for vain is the help of man. Through God we shall do valiantly, for it is He who shall tread down our enemies" (Psalm 60:11,12). Certainly cancer and coronary disease are real enemies.

The Bible says "You ask and do not receive, because you ask with wrong motives" (James 4:3 NASB). Our asking is always to be predicated upon God's will. To ask rightly is to ask according to His perfect will. We should want for ourselves and others only that which God in His infinite wisdom and foreknowledge knows is best. To pray and then leave the matter in God's hands is to experience deliverance from fear.

Fearing the Unknown

Those who have had cancer and have conquered this dread disease tell us that the fear settles deep within. It is a fear of all the unknowns that surround the disease, and for many victims it is a fear of the unknown future. What lies beyond death's door? But the Bible provides the answer to this fear. The Apostle Paul, in writing to young Timothy, his son in the faith, reminds him of the importance of taking care of his physical body, but then lays a greater emphasis on keeping spiritually fit. Both are important, but listen to the Apostle's words and be assured deep within that fear can be conquered:

> Train yourself toward godliness (piety)—keeping yourself spiritually fit.
>
> For physical training is of some value—useful for a little; but godliness [spiritual training] is useful and of value in everything and in every way, for it holds promise for the present life and also for the life which is to come.
> —1 Timothy 4:7b,8 AMP

FOOTNOTES

1. Dr. S.I. McMillen, *None of These Diseases* (Old Tappan, N.J.: Fleming H. Revell Co., 1963), p. 7.
2. Edith Schaeffer, *Affliction* (Old Tappan, N.J.: Fleming H. Revell Co., 1978), p. 21.
3. Ibid, p. 27.

10

> Good nutrition is not simp-
> ly what tastes good and
> looks good; but "good" is
> actually based on definite
> physiological mechanisms
> which encompass and
> directly affect each and
> every cell in the human
> body.
> —Dr. Harold W. Manner
> in *The Death of Cancer*[1]

Cell-Assurance Program

It doesn't make any difference whether you die like Elvis Presley because of a heart attack caused by clogged arteries, or whether you die like Howard Hughes because your kidneys are clogged. It is death either way. You cannot fool "mother nature"; you cannot defy the laws of God and hope to live a healthy and long life. Either we take care of these wonderful, beautiful bodies the Lord gave us or else we suffer the consequences. But we don't love our bodies in the right way. We wait until it is too late. You can't go to the hospital for a few days and get your health back just for the asking. No amount of medical care, regardless of how good and how costly it is, can give you future years.

Everyone carries within his body the potential for preventing cancer or a coronary. Good health and happy living are not accidents, although it does seem sometimes that people who pay no attention to their lifestyle have both. But appearing healthy and happy is not the same as obtaining total well-being, which includes spiritual, mental, and physical balance.

The tip of an iceberg should warn of the dangers below. Symptoms of ill health, however minor they may be, should clue us to the fact that the body is sending out warning signals. Healthy bodies, kept in metabolic balance, will be able to stand up under the stresses of living. The rudiments of well-balanced metabolic processes will prevent the cancer and coronary that kills.

Anticancer, Anticoronary: Your Own Personal Campaign Plan

If we are to survive, then we must take a fresh new look at preventing these chronic degenerative diseases. It is too late once they are well-established. As you plan your own personal anticancer and anticoronary campaign plan, you would do well to look at all the contributors of the functional breakdown of your cells. Bearing in mind what you have learned in preceding chapters, you will make determined efforts to avoid carcinogens such as cigarette smoke, chemicalized foods, and polluted air and water.

Where it is impossible to avoid these things, you will then do what is needed to help your body fight the toxins and that which contributes to cellular breakdown. Cancer prevention simply means a method whereby you keep your body healthy enough for its immune system to eliminate abnormal cellular growths as soon as they appear. What works in cancer prevention will work in preventing coronaries.

Prevention-oriented doctors understand that the only way we can really give the patient a fighting chance against cancer is to make conditions unfavorable for the growth of cancer cells, and favorable for the noncancer cells to be healthy enough to attack and control the cancer cells *anywhere* in the body. Surgery, radiation, and chemotherapy are believed to be stopgap measures. They do not overcome the *cause* of cancer, nor do they cure cancer. They kill some cancer cells and provide a temporary remission in most cases.

Often the real cause of the disease—which is, we believe,

sick cells that are growing without the usual body wisdom and control—goes undiagnosed and untreated. Any implied criticism of physicians is not intended, but this is written to help the individual reader help himself. God's plan is and always has been that we help ourselves to health and thus prevent the kind of carnage we are seeing in this country because of coronary and cancer.

Our Tranquilized Society

As you work at a personal anticancer and anticoronary campaign plan, you must come to grips with the effect of drugs on your body. This even includes the socially acceptable drugs —tranquilizers, weight-reducing pills, antihistamines, analgesics, barbiturates, antacids, water pills, cough medicines, hormones, sulfonamides, penicillins, erythromycin, as well as the many over-the-counter medications being used so freely today. Usually when we think of drug abuse, we think in terms of what we label "street" drugs—heroin, cocaine, "angel dust," marijuana, and hashish. But I submit to you that there is as much drug abuse among parents and adults as there is in the youth culture, although with different drugs.

It is no secret that for far too many people the answer to what they believe to be excess stress lies in a drug that has become almost a household word—Valium. The number of prescriptions written yearly runs at a rate of slightly less than 50 million, including refills, according to industry sources. Valium is the most widely prescribed drug in the country.[2] I have to agree with others who are sounding the warning that this is a considerable amount of "tranquilizing." Dr. Harold Harper and Michael Culbert *(How You Can Beat the Killer Diseases)* make the observation that "One might conclude that for the most part we are a tranquilized society awaiting death."

I have often stated that if all the tranquilizers were taken away from our society there would be such a national nervous breakdown that there wouldn't be enough well people to take care of the really sick people.

A doctor friend in Fort Worth, Texas, related to me that a woman patient of his was at a luncheon with seven other women. She received a phone call, and when she returned to the luncheon table, obviously distressed, all seven of her friends reached into their purses and offered her a Valium pill!

Oliver Wendell Holmes wrote in 1860 that ". . . if the whole materia medica, as now used, could be sunk to the bottom of the sea, it would be all the better for mankind—and all the worse for the fishes!" That may be amusing to read, but it's rather startling when you really think about it.

This is not to say that I am opposed to effective medical treatment and that I believe a return to the "good old days" would be better. Hardly! There is no denying that treatment today provides an effective range of drugs and procedures that are curative for a long list of diseases, and palliative for many more. But if there is to be major improvement of our national health, it will not come about through the use of drugs and medications, but it will come as doctors and health workers help people to understand the relationship between personal behavior and illness. We must be willing to accept the responsibility of maintaining our health.

Dr. John H. Knowles, President of The Rockefeller Foundation, in his book *Doing Better and Feeling Worse* (reporting on health in the United States), argues convincingly that the health of human beings is determined by their own behavior, their food, and the nature of their environment. "Over 99 percent of us are born healthy and made sick as a result of personal misbehavior and environmental conditions. The solution to the problems of ill health in modern American society involves individual responsibility, in the first instance, and social responsibility through public legislative and private voluntary efforts, in the second instance."[3]

Knowles and others of us will continue to beat the drums warning of the side effects of drugs. Knowles says, ". . . there is sufficient knowledge now to suggest that we should sharply restrict the use of many drugs."

Hooked on Alcohol?

There are many who take pride in the fact that they are not dependent on drugs. But many of these people are hooked on something else equally as bad, if not worse—they are drinking themselves into the grave. Perhaps someone reading this will take offense and say, "Now you're meddling. I could accept what you've had to say to this point, but back off— what I do in the privacy of my own home or when I'm out socializing is my business." It may be your business, but my business as a preventive-minded doctor is to declare the truth. To omit reference to the ill effects of alcohol on one's health would be a serious omission.

There is no use denying it—excessive use of alcohol is directly related to accidents and to liver disease (cirrhosis) as well as to a wide variety of other disorders, including vitamin deficiencies, inflammation of the pancreas, esophagus, and stomach, and muscular and neurologic diseases. Alcohol is a strong "risk factor" in cancer of the mouth, pharynx, larynx, and esophagus. Alcoholism in one or both parents is significantly associated with home injuries to children (more than 50 percent in some studies). The prevalence of "heavy-escape" drinkers in the United States has been estimated at 6.5 million people (5.4 percent of total adult population), and the figures for those who use alcohol chronically and excessively range up to 10 million adults. Teenage drinking is now nearly universal. A study of high-school students revealed that 36 percent reported getting drunk at least four times a year.[4]

We could fill up an entire book showing the bad effects of drinking, and refer you to hundreds of sources to document these statements. What does God have to say about this problem? (And that's what it is—a major problem.) This book is concerned with God's answer to cancer and coronary. One reference will suffice, although there are others.

> Wine is a mocker, strong drink is raging: and whosoever is deceived thereby is not wise.
> —Prov. 20:1

What is said about alcohol is being said about smoking, and we have already pointed out what smoking does to one's health. Everyone knows by now that cigarette smoking is a prime cause of lung cancer. Dr. Knowles points out that if we could figure out a way to get people to act on this single bit of information, we might have achieved a spectacular triumph in the prevention of deaths from cancer. Regrettably, that hasn't happened. "The same despairing thing can be said for the preventability of death from alcohol."[5]

Cell-Assurance Program

Your cell-assurance program should begin with adherance to what I call a nutrition-wise eating plan. Simply stated, that means getting into your daily diet as many of the better things as possible in your food. Preferably this will be natural food—uncooked raw fruits and vegetables to assure getting all those magic enzymes. If you cook nature's foods, then they should be steamed lightly for the shortest possible time. Your intake of meat should be curtailed in favor of eating more fish and fowl.

People ask me about eggs. The ordinary egg is one of the best food-dollar buys in today's supermarket. Eggs were carefully planned by our Creator to provide all the nourishment for the unhatched chick, so eggs are one of the most nutritionally complete foods. They contain nearly all the nutrients the body needs except vitamin C. Eggs are especially rich in all the B vitamins, and they are an excellent source of high-quality protein, trace minerals, phosphorous, and vitamins A, E, and K.

Are you wondering about the cholesterol controversy? This

has caused many people to shy away from eggs for fear of raising their cholesterol levels, inviting heart attacks. Recent investigations clearly indicate that eating cholesterol-rich food is not the real problem. As I wrote in a letter to the editor of the *Houston Post:* "I look forward to the day when the 'cholesterol cult' will have egg on their faces when they find out they have been 'egged on' by the minion of the sugar industry who are producing all our devitalized food—leading to the end product of poor metabolism and cholesterol. . . ."

Most of the cholesterol circulating in our bloodstreams is manufactured in the liver and in other body cells from what are called acetate radicles. Lecithin is a natural component which keeps cholesterol in suspension and cleanses the fat deposits which set up the conditions for a heart attack. And guess where lecithin is found? Eggs are rich in lecithin. To cut out eggs entirely could be counterproductive. The real culprits in our diet in America today are refined carbohydrates and white-flour products.

I tell my patients to enjoy eggs and to use them as nutrition-wise boosters in ground-meat dishes, appetizers, pancakes, waffles, sandwiches, salads, desserts, sauces, and homemade breads.

Convert Your Recipes

Many of your recipes can be converted to supply more of the needed nutrients and eliminate the disease-producing calories. By excluding hydrogenated (saturated) fats and processed carbohydrates from your recipes you will already have gone a long way in your efforts to be nutrition-wise. Become accustomed to substituting ingredients that are nutrition-boosters (for example, yogurt or blended cottage cheese for sour cream; wheat germ for bread crumbs).

Nutrition-Boosters

Brewers' yeast. Overcome the deficiencies of both processed and unprocessed foods by adding nutrient-rich brewers' yeast to as many foods as possible. Add brewers' yeast to: vegetable juices, soups, hamburgers, meat loaf, cereals, sandwich spreads, milk drinks, gravies, baked beans, applesauce, Spanish rice, meat, stews and hashes, cakes, cookies, muffins, pancakes, waffles, breads, biscuits (including all mixes).

Brewers' yeast may be purchased in powder or tablet form at groceries, drugstores, and health-food stores. Use as directed.

Powdered milk. Powdered skim milk contains over 36 percent protein of high biologic value. You can increase your protein, natural vitamins, and minerals (and also avoid the animal fat of whole milk) by adding skim-milk solids to your food as follows:

Scrambled eggs: *1 tablespoonful per egg.*
Custards, sauces, puddings: *Add 1 tablespoonful to the liquid in the recipe.*
Hamburger, meat loaf, and meat balls: *2 tablespoonfuls to each portion.*
Clear, canned, and homemade soups: *1 or 2 tablespoonfuls per bowl.*
Cooked cereals: *1 or 2 tablespoonfuls per serving.*
Gravies (no fat): *1 or 2 tablespoonfuls for thickening.*
Bread, cakes, muffins, cookies, pancake recipes, and mixes: *1 or 2 tablespoonfuls to standard recipe.*

Cottage cheese. This will be one of your best friends when you become nutrition-wise. A cup of cottage cheese yields slightly over 200 calories, most of them protein. You would have to drink 2½ pints of whole milk to get the same amount of protein, but you would also get over four times as many total calories. And about half of these would be fat calories.

A cup of cottage cheese (noncreamed) contains only 10 fat calories. An equal amount (in weight) of pork sausage (patties or links) contains 900 fat calories, or 90 times as much!

Cottage cheese can be used in these ways:

Add it to ground or chopped nuts, olives, onions, chives, pimento, chopped celery, chopped green or red peppers, shredded carrots, diced apples, dietetic jelly or preserves, chopped pickles, chopped or sliced hard-boiled eggs, chopped ham, leftover liver, liver paste, or diced dried beef for sandwich combinations.

Add cottage cheese to sauces, puddings, mayonnaise, salad dressings.

Use cottage cheese as a topping on gelatin and other molded desserts.

Add 1 tablespoon of cottage cheese for each egg to be scrambled. Add chipped beef, diced ham, or ground beef, and scramble the eggs.

Combine cottage cheese with spiced peaches or apple rings for a good accompaniment to meat or poultry dishes.

Whip cottage cheese in a tomato or bouillon aspic.

Heap cottage cheese onto honeydew, casaba, or cantaloupe halves for breakfast, or as a first or last course for main meals.

Use cottage cheese as the base for a cooked sauce over Brussels sprouts, asparagus, broccoli, boiled onions, green beans, and carrots.

Fill big, ripe, red tomatoes or green-pepper halves with cottage cheese for added protein calories. Serve cottage cheese as a main dish, seasoned with vinegar, cinnamon, nutmeg, or favorite herbs and spices. Top with slivered almonds or lemon juice.

Add cottage cheese to any sauces and salad dressings to proteinize them.

Blend cottage cheese with lemon juice, buttermilk, or yogurt for a low-calorie, high-protein, nutrition-wise sour cream.

Combine low-calorie jams, jellies, or preserves with cottage cheese for your breakfast toast.

Enhance the flavor and nutrient value of a dish of cottage cheese with honey and wheat germ for a light lunch.

Pile cottage cheese on pieces of pineapple, sliced halved peaches, or apricots for added protein calories.

Try a cottage cheese omelet, or fill pancakes with cottage cheese and low-calorie jam or preserves for a festive and nutritious brunch.

Add cottage cheese to pancakes, muffins, cakes, and cookies to step up your protein calories.

Whip cottage cheese with butter flavoring and saffron for coloring for a low-calorie spread. Vegetable oil may be added.

Whip cottage cheese into butter or margarine to increase its protein content.

Use cottage cheese, whipped and seasoned, as a baked potato topper.

Use cottage cheese, gelatin, and noncaloric sweetener to make a low-calorie cheesecake.

Use cottage cheese as a base for raw vegetable dips.

Top fish, seafood, beef, veal, chicken, or turkey with whipped and seasoned cottage cheese.

Use cottage cheese as you would cream cheese in cake or muffins, toppings or frostings, cocktail spreads, and molded salads.

Whip cottage cheese with canned evaporated skim milk and sweeten with noncaloric artificial sweetener to taste for use as a substitute for whipped cream.

Fresh or canned orange juice and other fruit juices can flavor cottage cheese dishes.

Mix 1 cup of cottage cheese with chopped nuts, celery, diced green peppers, raisins, pimento, chopped olives, or diced hard-boiled eggs for tasty variety.

Gelatin. Unflavored gelatin is another nutritional friend. It is all protein. However, it lacks the essential amino acid tryptophan, and should be mixed or eaten with some animal protein for full effectiveness.

Do not confuse unflavored gelatin with the sweetened and flavored brand-name gelatins. They are 85 percent sugar.

Unflavored gelatin is excellent as a thickening agent. It can be used for all types of aspics, jellied soups, and consommes, or added, without jelling, to bouillon, tea, or coffee for a nutritious hot beverage.

Gelatin can be mixed with cold drinks, such as fruit juices, milk, and vegetable juices, but must be stirred and drunk quickly before it jells.

Add gelatin to puddings, custards, whips, fluffs, snows, and creams for more healthful dessert dishes.

Liver. Liver is such a nutritious food that you should include it in your menu at least once or twice a week. It is an excellent source of protein and of all the B-complex vitamins. It is also a good source of vitamin A. Do not overcook it or it will lose its precious nutrients.

Dice or chop any kind of liver (beef, calf, pork, lamb, or chicken) and mix it into meat patties, meatloaf, or meatballs.

Grind cooked liver into a liver paste to use as a sandwich or cracker spread.

Liquefy a small amount of raw liver in a blender and add it to vegetable, fruit, or milk drinks.

If you don't care for cooked liver, substitute powdered desiccated liver, obtainable from a drugstore or health-food store. Add a small amount to drinks, hamburgers, and meatloaves.

Wheat germ. Wheat germ is a rich source of unsaturated fatty acids, the B-complex vitamins, vitamin E, minerals, and protein. If it is processed or toasted, it loses most of its previous vitamin E, and if not kept refrigerated, will soon become rancid and unusable.

Fortify many of your foods and menus by using wheat germ in the following ways:

Cereals, hot or cold: *Add 1 tablespoonful to each portion.*
Soup: *Add 1 or 2 tablespoonfuls to each serving. Wheat germ can be used to thicken clear soups.*

Salads: *Add to taste to mixed green or molded salads.*
Hamburgers, meat loaf: *Add 1 or 2 tablespoonfuls per serving.*
Cream gravy: *2 tablespoonfuls of wheat germ.*
Vegetable juices: *Add 1 teaspoonful per 4-ounce glass.*

Soybean products. Soybeans contain all the essential amino acids in good proportions and are one of the few nonanimal proteins that are considered to be complete. They also contain lecithin, which helps to reduce high cholesterol levels in the blood.

Defatted soybean flour is considered high in digestibility, nearly as high as meat, eggs, and milk. It contains goodly amounts of iron, calcium, and other nutrient minerals and is high in vitamins.

Soy flour can be added to many foods to increase their nutritional content.

Add soy flour to wheat or rye flour for making bread. Since soy flour does not contain gluten (an elastic protein substance that gives cohesiveness to dough), it can only replace 10 to 12 percent of the wheat or rye flour in bread recipes.

Soybean milk can be used by those who are allergic to cow's milk or for cardiac patients on low-sodium diets.

Soy cheese, or tofu, can be used as a good source of protein.

Vegetarians should include soybean products in their diets as substitutes for meat proteins.

Lecithin. Lecithin is a relatively tasteless, water-soluble granular powder made from defatted soybeans. It is a component of all living cells and plays a vital role in the biochemistry of the body.

Lecithin is an emulsifying agent that tends to break up large fat globules into smaller droplets that can be utilized better by the body. It appears to have a cholesterol-lowering effect on patients with high blood-cholesterol levels. Cholesterol increases in the blood when lecithin levels drop.

Dr. Lester Morrison and his associates in Los Angeles have used lecithin as adjunctive therapy in the prevention and treatment of arteriosclerosis and heart conditions, and they find that it has great value in reducing high cholesterol levels.

Physicians who prescribe lecithin recommend 4 to 6 tablespoonfuls a day when cholesterol levels are high, and then 1 or 2 tablespoonfuls a day to maintain low levels and prevent the ravages of clogged arteries.

Use granular lecithin in milk and vegetable or fruit juices. Or add it to sandwich spreads.

Evaporated skim milk. The addition of canned evaporated skim milk to foods and beverages is a fast and easy way of stepping up their nutrient content. It is an excellent source of all the proteins, minerals, and B-vitamins that occur in evaporated and whole milk, but without the fat (butterfat) calories. It differs from powdered milk only in water content.

Evaporated skim milk stores easily, keeps well, and is a convenient emergency food. It's a good idea to keep a supply of it on hand at all times.

Augment the protein, vitamin, and mineral content of these foods by using evaporated skim milk instead of regular evaporated or whole milk: scrambled eggs, hamburgers, meatloaf, meatballs, cooked cereals, dips, whips, appetizer spreads, sandwich spreads, molded salads, aspics, sauces, salad dressings, breads, waffles, pancakes, cakes, cookies, toppings, frostings, beverages, gravies, custards, and puddings.

Listen to Your Body Talk

As you begin your cell-assurance diet and program, you will want to develop the habit of listening to your body talk. Signs of poor cell function would include the following:

low energy level and a general feeling of listlessness
depression and frequent moodiness
inadequate stamina and endurance
flatulence (gas)
malfunction such as constipation and diarrhea
pain (frequent headaches, joint and muscle pain)
insomnia
circulatory problems such as leg cramps, shortness
of breath, numbness of hands or feet, coldness of
extremities
scalp, hair, and skin problems
nausea
anxiety, irritability, impatience
hostility
overweight

Make a list of your symptoms and problems which might indicate an impoverished cell state. Use the list to monitor the progress of your cell-assurance program. Realize, however, that it takes time to overcome deficiencies and to bring about a metabolic balance. Don't give up. As the saying goes, "It's always too soon to quit."

Overweight?

It is wise to know what your blood-sugar levels are and to have them checked on a continuing basis. You should weigh yourself regularly, and if you are overweight you should begin immediately to reduce your total caloric intake. If you decrease your calories considerably and increase your caloric expenditure by increased exercise such as walking, then it is reasonable to expect that you will begin to lose weight. Count the calories you expend. As an example, 500 calories a day difference can make a pound of fat in one week.

Exercise and Caloric Energy Output

Exercise must be a part of your cell-power program, but it

must be in moderation and in proper relationship to your energy and nutrient reserves. Many persons tend to overdo because they think that overexercising will immediately provide the results they want to achieve. But we recommend exercise in moderation, working your way into a total program, taking into account your age, your work, your general health, and other factors.

Exercise should be progressive, and we consider walking and swimming to be your best way of improving circulation and toning and firming muscles. Many exercise programs are available in connection with gym classes and the YMCA. For a price many spas have fine machines that can be used to improve circulation and strengthen muscles. You can use a stationary bicycle and a moderate exercise calisthenics program of your own in your home with very beneficial results.

Self-discipline is the key, along with consistency. It is important to remember that the *quantity* of blood that helps your cells must have the *quality* that is adequate for proper cell functions.

Oxygen is so vital to our metabolic and energy needs that deep-breathing exercises should be performed many times during the day. Here is what we recommend:

Stand with feet far apart. Extend arms from shoulder-level sideways.

A.   Bend forward, exhaling through your mouth slowly and completely. Touch right fingertips to left foot. Keep knees as straight as possible.

B.   Return to original position; raise arms and lean backward as far as you can while inhaling very deeply through your nose. Contract and pull in abdominal muscles. Maintain until you have to exhale.

C.   Bend forward, exhaling through the mouth very slowly, and touch left fingertips to right foot.

D.   Return to original position. Repeat abdominal muscle contraction and deep breathing.

Before undertaking any new strenuous exercise program, it is the better part of wisdom to see your doctor and get his evaluation of your general state of health. A word of caution about overextending yourself: a too-zealous program can have adverse effects. We have all read or heard of joggers dropping dead. Generally speaking, an exercise program should not produce excess fatigue (fatigue that doesn't clear up after a few minutes of rest).

The following charts should be helpful as you determine what is best for you.

APPROXIMATE CALORIES USED PER HOUR ACCORDING TO BODY WEIGHT

ACTIVITY	100 lbs.	120 lbs.	140 lbs.	160 lbs.	180 lbs.	200 lbs.
1. Sleeping	.45	.50	.65	.70	.80	.85
2. Awake but lying down	.50	.60	.70	.80	.80	1.00
3. Sitting quietly or eating	.65	.80	.90	1.05	1.15	1.30
4. Reading aloud, writing, standing, or sewing	.70	.85	.95	1.10	1.25	1.40
5. Dressing and undressing	.75	.90	1.05	1.20	1.35	1.50
6. Singing	.80	.95	1.10	1.25	1.40	1.60
7. Driving a car or typewriting rapidly	.90	1.10	1.25	1.45	1.65	1.80
8. Ironing, cooking, dishwashing, or dusting	.95	1.10	1.30	1.50	1.65	1.85
9. Light exercise, gardening	1.10	1.30	1.55	1.75	2.00	2.20
10. Walking slowly (2.6 mph)	1.30	1.55	1.80	2.10	2.35	2.60
11. Carpentry, metal work	1.55	1.90	2.20	2.50	2.80	3.10
12. "Active exercise" (e.g., bowling)	1.90	2.25	2.65	3.00	3.40	3.75
13. Walking moderately fast (3.75 mph)	1.95	2.35	2.75	3.10	3.50	3.90

ACTIVITY	100 lbs.	120 lbs.	140 lbs.	160 lbs.	180 lbs.	200 lbs.
14. Walking downstairs	2.35	2.85	3.30	3.80	4.25	4.70
15. "Severe" exercise	2.90	3.50	4.10	4.65	5.25	5.95
16. Swimming	3.25	3.90	4.55	5.20	5.85	6.50
17. Running (5.4 mph)	3.70	4.45	5.20	5.90	6.65	7.40
18. "Very severe" exercise	3.90	4.70	5.45	6.25	7.00	7.80
19. Walking very fast (5.3 mph)	4.20	5.05	5.90	6.75	7.60	8.45
20. Walking upstairs	7.20	8.60	10.05	11.50	12.90	14.35

EXAMPLE
100-POUND WOMAN'S CALORIC EXPENDITURE

ACTIVITY	Body Weight		Calories Per Lb.		Time	Total Calories Used
Sleep	100	x	.45	x	8 hrs.	360
Housekeeping	100	x	.95	x	8 hrs.	760
Grooming	100	x	.75	x	1 hr.	75
Reading	100	x	.70	x	1 hr.	70
Watching TV	100	x	.65	x	2 hrs.	130
Meal activity	100	x	.65	x	1 hr.	65
Driving car	100	x	.85	x	1 hr.	85
Light exercise	100	x	1.10	x	2 hrs.	220
					DAILY TOTAL	1765

Shelf-Control

No, that was not a typographical error. You must exercise *shelf*-control. That is one of the best exercises you can perform to prevent disease and to fight the battle of the bulge. This means that when you venture forth to the supermarket you will not buy anything that will contribute to poor health. If you exercise shelf-control you will not put yourself or other family members on the shelf.

You will organize your shopping and your kitchen to implement your newly acquired knowledge of nutrition. You will gradually equip your kitchen with a quality juicer, slicer, shredder or food chopper, thermometer, postal scale (to familiarize yourself with portion values of foods), and other items that will make preparing food a challenge and a joy.

You will decrease "malignant," disease-producing calories found in processed carbohydrate foods. This means that you may have to go through your kitchen junking the junk foods that are already there. This means getting rid of white flour and white-flour products (white bread, macaroni, noodles, lasagna, spaghetti), and refined white sugar and sugar products (including pastries, gelatin, candy bars, ice cream, etc.) You will also eliminate chewing gum. Ever since my high-school days I have remembered what our music teacher said (in an effort to discourage the chewing of gum): "Gum-chewing girls and boys and cud-chewing cows are alike, and yet there's a difference somehow—it's the intelligent look on the face of the cow."

You will please your husband and children with foods like "Mother used to make" without the wrong calories which are conducive to the development of disease.

You will diligently work to increase the protein, vitamin, mineral, and unsaturated-fatty-acid content of the foods you buy and prepare.

You will learn to lesson total caloric intake to prevent fat from shortening your lives.

You will stay away from refined vegetable oils (which are saturated), and instead will use corn oil, peanut oil, cottonseed oil, or safflower-seed oil. You will therefore minimize butter, fats, and grease in your diets. For cooking, you will use heavy skillets and griddles that require no grease or oil. You should broil more of your meats, fish, and fowl.

You will use salt sparingly.

You must guide and indoctrinate your children so they will eat foods that build good teeth, bones, and healthy bodies.

You will teach them the dangers of soft drinks and junk-food snacks.

You will learn to understand labels on food products in order to avoid misunderstandings regarding contents of packages, cans, and containers of food.

You will consult the yellow pages of your phone book for jobbers and distributors of food products conducive to good health. You can contact your county agent, state farm bureau, or nearby agricultural colleges for information about organic food supplies and mills offering whole-grain flours and cereals for sale.

You will stock only those items on your pantry shelf and in your refrigerator and freezer that are of high nutritional quality. And you will not compromise.

You will remember at all times that you are the custodian of your own and your family's health. Your aim will be to attain a superior level of health for all of you, and to thereby prevent disease.

You will recognize the importance of water as an essential nutrient, and you will see to it that your family consumes adequate amounts of distilled water or spring water or tested well-water as much as possible.

You will eat more nuts and seeds, which provide essential fatty acids and high-quality protein.

You will eat only breads and cereals of the whole-wheat variety, and then in moderation (since they are carbohydrates).

Prevention of disease simply means forsaking your bad habits. The elimination of cancer alone would mean that one out of six people would live 10.8 years longer.

We predispose ourselves to heart attacks, strokes, cancer of the gastrointestinal tract, diabetes, liver and gall-bladder disease, and degenerative arthritis of the hips, knees, and ankles mainly because of our bad nutritional habits. It is estimated that 16 percent of Americans under the age of 30 are obese, while 40 percent of the total population, or 80 million Americans, are 20 or more pounds above the ideal weight for their height, sex, and age. Over 30 percent of all men between 50 and 59 years are 20 percent overweight and 20 percent are at least 10 percent overweight.[6] Dietary factors play a major role in cardiovascular disease and cancer.

Studies of nearly 7000 adults for 5½ years showed that life expectancy and health are significantly related to the following basic health habits:

1) three meals a day at regular times
2) breakfast every day
3) moderate exercise two or three times a week
4) adequate sleep, (7 or 8 hours a night)
5) no smoking
6) moderate weight
7) no alcohol

A 45-year-old man who practices 0-3 of these habits has a remaining life expectancy of 21.6 years (to age 67), while one with 6-7 of these habits has a life expectancy of 33.1 years (to age 78). In other words, 11 years could be added to life expectancy by relatively simple changes in habits of living! It has also been found, as a result of these studies, that the health status of those who practiced all seven habits was similar to people 30 years younger who observed none of these habits.[7,8]

FOOTNOTES

1. Dr. Harold W. Manner, *The Death of Cancer* (Evanston, Ill.: Advanced Century Publishing Co., 1978), p. 148.
2. Brian Sullivan, "Many Valium Users Ignorant of Drug's Effect," in *The Courier News,* Bridgewater, N.J., April 2, 1979.
3. John H. Knowles, M.D., *Doing Better and Feeling Worse* (New York: W.W. Norton & Co., 1977), p. 58.
4. Ibid., p. 63.
5. Ibid., p. 45.
6. Ibid., p. 63.
7. Ibid., pp. 61, 62.
8. The following companies will supply products to physicians after summary of cell-assurance program.

   Biotics
   5731 Savoy Lane
   Houston, Texas 77036

   Standard Process Laboratories, Inc.
   2023 West Wisconsin Avenue
   P.O. Box 652
   Milwaukee, Wisconsin 53201

   VM Nutri-Food, Inc.
   P.O. Box 286
   1012 Host Drive
   Lake Geneva, Wisconsin 53147

   Nutri-Dyn Products Corporation
   5705 West Howard Street
   Niles, Illinois 60648

   Seroyal Brands, Inc.
   P.O. Box 6500
   Concord, California 94524

   DaVinci Laboratories
   1 Executive Drive
   Burlington, Vermont 05401

11

It can be concluded that Supernutrition, which stresses higher-than-average intake of vitamins and minerals, most probably reduces the incidence of cancer.
—Richard A. Passwater in *Super-Nutrition*

Nutrition Plus

In this "game of life" (so-called by some) we are fools indeed if we do not play to win. We know we can't live forever on this planet, but who wants to die an agonizingly painful death because of cancer or some other degenerative disease! Food may support life, but it does not necessarily sustain health. What then is the answer?

The answer is in what I call the protective, preventive power of a supertherapeutic augmentation of concentrated nutrients. This is nutrition plus. It consists of a good nutrition program as outlined in the preceding chapter plus the use of nutrition-boosters and supplementing one's diet with vitamin and mineral nutrients.

As far as the medical profession is concerned, supplementing one's diet this way is intensely controversial. I do not believe that vitamins and minerals are a cure-all, but I do recognize that even a well-planned diet by a conscientious homemaker might be deficient in certain essential nutrients.

It takes time to cultivate a taste for foods that are nutritionally superior. Most people have become so accustomed to the denaturalized and processed foods that they are easily discouraged and inclined to give up. Perhaps we need to remind ourselves of what the book of Proverbs says. There we read: "When you sit down to dine . . . consider carefully what is before you; and put a knife to your throat if you are a man of great appetite. Do not desire his delicacies, for it is deceptive food (Proverbs 23:1-3 NASB). There is silent violence in our foods, and for this reason we need to fortify our bodies with the vitamins and minerals that are all-essential.

Let's get one thing straight—controversy in the medical profession is nothing new. The history of science is a chronicle of controversies. Medical history records stories of men of science who were harassed and even removed from the faculties of universities, men who were laughed at and ridiculed, and medical contemporaries who were angered at these "radical" researchers and their findings. And yet today many of those men and women are hailed as heroes and heroines, and their discoveries are marked as dramatic turning points in the quest for overcoming disease.

Doctors should not be considered nutrition experts. One writer describes them as "body repairmen." They are hard-working, dedicated, and disciplined. We should never underestimate their intelligence or their devotion to their profession. They spend years acquiring the knowledge that will enable them to diagnose illness, administer drugs, and perform surgical procedures. But the busyness of those years of study precludes an emphasis on studying nutrition. Moreover, most medical doctors will tell you that the teaching received in medical school on the subject of nutrition was woefully inadequate. This is not to imply that the average physician is a nutrition imbecile. But it is to recognize his limitations in an area for which he has often not received adequate training. Usually his main deterrent is the probable criticism of his equally uninformed colleagues.

Some researchers believe that more than half a million Americans die prematurely each year because of insufficient nutrition. This does not mean they were underfed, but it does mean they were not *well-fed*. What does that say to you about the prevalent attitude among the medical profession, who tell you that supplementing your diet is not necessary because you get what you need in your food?

Illness Medicine

Traditional medicine is, as more than one holistic physician will tell you, just "illness medicine." Modern medicine is mostly crisis-oriented. Specialists in the field of medicine abound. This is treatment aimed at one part of the patient's body rather than the total human being. Unfortunately, when this happens, the person as such is given little consideration. Essential to total health is the harmonious balance of the body, mind, and spirit. This produces the symphony of wellness discussed in an earlier chapter. This is not to diminish the importance of specialists, but it is to point to the need for you to take charge of yourself so that when and if disease rears its ugly head, you will be in a position to relate to that one who is administering help to you just where you sense something may have gone wrong.

To permit others to dictate our health maintenance lifestyle on the basis of partial information at best (often received from our case histories by someone other than the administering physician) is most unwise. You are more than a diseased gall bladder, more than a murmuring heart, more than a diabetic. You are a whole person.

What is needed for the greatest possible good of all of us is an open-mindedness by both the medical profession as well as the individual he is endeavoring to treat. Dogmatic opinions will not pave the way for possibilities of change. Amazing breakthroughs have occurred, particularly in recent years, in discoveries of the importance of concentrated nutrients to renewed health. But the average doctor will still tell you, if you ask his advice about supplementing your diet, that 1) vitamins and minerals really aren't necessary, since you get what you need in your food; 2) taking concentrated nutrients won't hurt you if you read the labels, but it's really a waste of money; and 3) drugs will get the job done more effectively and faster.

Without seeming to come down too hard on the medical profession, let me remind you, the reader, that the pharmaceutical industry works hand in glove with the medical profession. The professed aim is to treat the patient but more often it is the symptoms of disease that are being treated while the patient as a whole person is overlooked. What contributed to the breakdown of that person's health to begin with? Traditionally the doctor asks you some questions about how you feel, where it hurts, how long you have had the symptoms, etc. X-rays may follow, plus tests. Then follows the prescription for medication and, hopefully, within a short space of time you begin to feel better. The question is, how long does that "feeling better" last? Was the cause remedied? Will the cure last?

Over half of America's population is currently afflicted with degenerative diseases that generally began at an early age and progressed to an inevitable crisis, with perhaps some treatment along the way, but with little or no effort to get at the root cause. No major lifestyle change has been recommended, nor have suggestions been made as to how the patient could improve the quality of his living by knowing the principles of balanced nutrition and the role of vitamin-nutrients and mineral-nutrients and other factors as discussed in previous chapters in this book.

An open-minded look at the facts, then, is in order. We have been busy stuffing our faces for years with all the goodies offered by the food industries, but in the process we have been creating nutrient deficiencies both in ourselves and in our children that are resulting in degenerative diseases and serious illnesses that will surface later. If they have not yet surfaced for somebody, all indications and current health findings point to the clearly recognizable fact that dietary intake is a gross contributor to ill health and for many people an untimely death.

Dr. Edith Weir of the USDA maintains that if the public adhered to a diet which achieved the recommended daily allowance (RDA) of the USDA, 300,000 deaths could be prevented each year from heart disease and stroke, and another 150,000 deaths could be prevented each year from cancer. (Those were 1971 findings.) She estimated that if all diets were improved to RDA levels, there would be dramatic improvements in at least 19 major health problems.[1]

If people followed a nutrition-wise program, the following things could happen in this country:

1. Heart disease could be reduced by 60-80 percent.
2. Cancer could be reduced by 30-40 percent.
3. Air-pollution damage to the human body could be reduced by 95 percent.
4. The cure rate for schizophrenia could be increased by 500 percent.
5. Arthritis and other crippling diseases could be reduced by 40 percent.
6. The incidence and severity of all types of diseases could be reduced by 40 percent.[2]

What About RDAs and Minimum Daily Requirements (MDRs)?

A large number of scientists, nutritionists, and doctors agree with the analysis of Dr. Roger J. Williams *(Nutrition Against Disease* and *Nutrition in a Nutshell)*: "When we speak of average diets or minimum daily requirements, we are using broad terms which are unrealistic with respect to anyone's individual eating problems. We need to recognize that each individual's problem is based upon his or her own requirements, which are not set by any committee. To understand these requirements, we must think in terms of what the various nutrients do when they enter our bodies and of the organs and tissues they affect.''[3]

Sadly, millions of people are being misled by the Food and Drug Administration (FDA), the American Medical Association (AMA) and their personal physicians into believing that, if they follow the USDA's recommended daily allowance (RDA) or minimum daily requirements (MDR), they would not need to augment their diets with concentrated nutrients. But even following these recommendations (which so many people do not, as has been pointed out) would provide no guarantee that you were getting what your individual biochemical makeup required.

Body Wisdom: How Do You Develop It?

There is nothing that can take the place of an intelligent understanding of your body's functions. To shrug your shoulders and scoff at those who try to incite your interest in the subject is to write across your health certificate, "INDIFFERENCE and IGNORANCE BY CHOICE contributed to my demise.''

It is granted that food faddists exist and that some of their recommendations leave a great deal to be desired. Oversimplification of one's health problems is not going to restore health to anyone. Succumbing to the extremes or the errors of food faddism is not the right approach. You need to develop a sensitivity to your body's signals.

The body has a wisdom all its own. When it is assaulted by that which is disagreeable to your system it's going to let you know in one or more ways. That should be a flashing light that warns you not to eat that particular food or combination of foods again. Stop and think! What was it you ate that made you feel so uncomfortable? Eliminate that from your diet.

"Tell Me, Doctor, What Really Are Vitamins?"

Vitamins are actually food substances essential to life. As was pointed out in the chapter on enzymes, they are utilized in the body as coenzymes—catalysts for physiological response by the body to the effects of stress. The human body does not make vitamins; we have to rely on getting them from our food. If we do not obtain them in sufficient quantities for normal functioning of the body, there will eventually occur what I call cellular crisis (which, as has been emphasized, is the contributing factor to cancer and degenerative diseases).

It is good preventive practice to be sure that one's diet is adequate in these vital elements by taking therapeutic augmentation of concentrated nutrients. No one is immune from risk factors in our society which effect our physical and mental well-being. If we choose to ignore these risk factors, then we must accept the penalties. Nature in its infinite wisdom cannot be defied.

The alternative is to use all of the protective, preventive measures that are now known and available to us. God has given us the ability to exert positive action. God's normal plan for the body is health, not sickness. This being true, the clear-cut admonition from the Apostle Paul bears repeating: "Therefore, glorify God in your body" (1 Corinthians 6:20).

There are natural vitamins, synthetic vitamins, and organic vitamins.

Natural vitamins are those which exist in nature rather than being artificially produced. Actually they are a concentrated food, the source being plant or animal. They may contain other essential nutrients, such as enzymes, synergists, catalysts, minerals, proteins, or unidentified nutrients.

Synthetic vitamins are exactly what the name implies—

man-made, artificially produced substances with the same molecular bond as the living form of food. These are the vitamins you generally find in drug and grocery stores.

Organic vitamins are similar to natural vitamins except that they are from "organically grown" (pesticide-free) plant sources.

The reader is no doubt already knowledgeable enough to know that the natural and organic food supplements are sold by better health food stores and private distributors. They cost more, but in long-range effectiveness their benefits far outweigh their additional cost.

Good Body Ecology

We hear much about pollution of the atmosphere, and we are cautioned about polluting the landscape, but we hear very little about good body ecology. To fight self-pollution is every individual's own peculiar responsibility. It is not something we can arbitrarily abdicate to society or someone else and then heap the blame upon them when something goes wrong. The only exception to this might be a youngster who must rely on what his parents feed him.

It's not so much what we *do* eat, but what we *don't* eat that spells the difference between radiant good health and a mediocre state of health (or outright failing health). The body has an amazing ability to heal itself when given proper nutrition, but that will not go on indefinitely. For some people cellular weakness begins sooner than for others, with the onslaught of disease right around the corner. We bring on these debilitating diseases through improper lifestyles, and of course our deteriorating environment contributes to this as well. The fact remains that the body cannot get values which we don't put into our mouths.

If you treat your body fairly, the potential for a healthy, mentally alert, long life exists.

Vitamania

Isolation of individual nutrients and the study of their deficiency records have stimulated the drug and chemical industries to make synthetic chemicals similar to individual natural nutrients. I have referred to these as *synthetic vitamins.* As a result of this, "chemical cocktails" and "concoctions" of chemical combinations line the shelves of our stores today. It is true that many people have developed what I call "vitamania." "You should take a few vitamins," is the stock selling phrase. We have a lot of part-smart people.

That is why, to some extent, I back off from overworking the words *vitamins* and *minerals.* You will note that I refer instead to concentrated nutrients or vitamin-nutrients and mineral-nutrients. It becomes apparent that we need new and better thinking and understanding about our bodies' needed nutrient requirements. As previously mentioned, we have in this country a state I call *anutrientosis,* which signifies a lack of *many* nutrients. (This replaces the old idea that a deficiency state is a lack of one individual nutrient.) Anutrientosis stresses the state of a multiple nutrient-deficiency state. It relates to more advanced thinking about applied medical nutrition.

When you stop and consider that about 45 nutrients are required in optimum quantities daily to maintain excellent health, you begin to realize the complexity of what we are talking about and the probability that your diet—however well and beautifully prepared—is not supplying all that is needed for optimum health.

In the field of preventive medicine, advanced thinking causes us to realize that not only do we have to think in terms of anutrientosis, but we must also realize that many necessary nutrients which are left in our highly processed foods are often negated by the addition of adulterant chemicals.

So we have coined another new word to point out that we are adding more bodily damage by the effects of *antinutri-*

tion. Consider all the environmental factors that are dangerous and damaging to the amounts of proper nutrients left in our food and our environment today, and you will begin to understand the meaning of antinutrition—that which contributes to lessen the value of the nutrients left in our food as well as adding the effects of illness-producing "chemical pollution."

All of this brings us right back to our originally stated belief that our state of ill health today is because we have cells which are sick and unable to metabolize efficiently. Because they are unable to rid themselves of all the end products of poor metabolism we have a cell state that I call *cell pollution*. The point is that the addition of these needed nutrients to your daily intake can improve your physical well-being dramatically by increasing your cell power.

There is no doubt that *all* vitamins and minerals play an important role in the health of the body; any program to resist cancer, coronary, and degenerative diseases must include all these vital nutrients through an optimum nutrition plan and the use of concentrated nutrients in pill or tablet form.

Health Preservers

While many individuals are vitamin conscious, fewer are aware of the need for minerals. Vitamins are not the only thing necessary to optimum health; minerals are also tremendously significant. There are those who insist, just as they do with vitamins, that we get all the minerals we need in the foods we consume. As has already been pointed out, these valuable vitamin and mineral nutrients are often lost through food processing. The importance of choosing raw fruits and vegetables over canned and processed cannot be overemphasized. Foods grown on mineral-rich earth (through organic gardening) will supply what we need, provided that they have not received spraying with pesticides or chemical fertilizers, which lessen the mineral content of many foods.

If we are going to build a house we must have all the supplies that are necessary. A house requires a roof; if you use a shingle roof, you need shingle nails. Windows and doors require knobs, hinges, weights, and proper framing. To build a house, the carpenter utilizes all the essential building materials. Just so in our bodies. The body has multiple functions and requires in varying amounts the vitamins, minerals, carbohydrates, fats, proteins, and water for optimum body functioning.

Therapeutic augmentation of concentrated nutrients means that we are getting all the things the body needs, including minerals. You should never underestimate the importance of minerals to your total well-being. Minerals have been appropriately called "building stones." Minerals may be defined as inorganic, crystalline, and homogeneous (having similarity in structure because of common descent) chemicals.

Actually the mineral content of foods is rather miniscule. On the basis of comparison of relative amounts of minerals in the body, one might be tempted to conclude that minerals are of very limited significance in the human body. But nothing could be further from the truth. Some of the unique and necessary roles which minerals as a group perform in the body are: 1) controllers of water balance, 2) regulators of acid-base balance, 3) structural components, 4) constituents of enzymes, hormones, and other key compounds, and 5) catalysts for various reactions in the body.

Minerals that are classified as macronutrients (needed in large amounts) include calcium, phosphorous, sodium, potassium, and magnesium. Those required in lesser quantities are called micronutrients (or trace minerals) and include iron, iodine, molybdenum, copper, selenium, zinc, manganese, chromium, and tin.

When God instructed Adam and Eve how to care for their bodies and how to survive, He gave them the most elemental instructions. "Look!" God said, "I have given you the seed-bearing plants throughout the earth, and all the fruit trees for your food'' (Genesis 1:29 TLB). God, who formed us from the dust of the earth, knew that all the elements in the soil necessary for the building of a totally healthy body were there to begin with. The Creator, with infinite wisdom, neglected nothing.

Ancient peoples as well as peoples living today in Western Europe, the Balkan countries, Turkey, and certain lesser-known areas of the world today exist largely on the very things that God Himself instructed the first man and woman to eat. These are people who are noted for their longevity and disease-free living. Sprouts, seeds, and nuts are used much by such people and are rich in mineral content, but they are sadly lacking in many diets today.

Chelation Therapy

If minerals are to be absorbed into the body they must be in contact with protein in the stomach and intestines. Not all minerals are absorbed as they should be, for varying reasons. This creates absorption problems. Morton Walker explains the problem:

> To move the minerals into your cells they must be chelated with protein. The chelating agents of the body, usually amino acids, surround the mineral molecules and grasp them like crab claws. This protects them from chemical reactions with other minerals and permits absorption through the gut wall by the amino acids' paving the way. *Amino acids* are the building blocks of all proteins.[4]

A comparatively new procedure has come to the attention of health-conscious individuals in recent years. This process, called *chelation therapy,* has been used successfully in reducing deposits of calcium in the arteries and in other parts of the body. Dr. H. Ray Evers *(Let's Live,* March 1978) has used the process in treating over 7000 patients and has given over 150,000 doses of endrate (the chelating substance) without any trouble and with good results. He describes it as a process "in which we are only improving circulation and trying to improve nutrition and oxygenation so the tissues may be fed in the proper manner and the normal chemical reactions may take place inside the cells."

Many dramatic accounts have been documented where individuals feel that their lives have literally been handed back to them as a result of chelation therapy after they had been pronounced as good as dead. Norm and Virginia Rohrer *(How to Eat Right and Feel Great)* relate the account of a school administrator who had a massive coronary but whose life was spared after chelation therapy. Morton Walker describes several similar accounts in his book *Total Health*.

The amino acid used in chelation is called ethylene diamine tetraacetic acid (EDTA). It is dropped into the bloodstream and flows through the blood vessels and picks up ionized calcium floating around. In the individual suffering from atherosclerosis, in which the artery walls are severely narrowed because of being filled with plaque (deposits of cholesterol, blood fat, and calcium), the plaque disintegrates as the man-made chelating agent unblocks the obstructed arteries. It has been described as cleaning out clogged blood vessels in much the way a septic engineer unclogs your home septic system.

The question is asked, "How do you get rid of the calcium?" Like a lobster's or crab's claw, the amino acid clamps down on the offending metals or mineral deposits and chelates (carries) them to the kidneys and out the urinary tract. How do you get rid of the offenders? You urinate them away.

About a thousand physicians are offering the treatment in this country (write Academy of Medical Preventics, 2811 "L" Street, Sacramento, California 95816 for list).

Intravenous chelation therapy has come under attack from the AMA, which is not surprising. The pharmaceutical industry and the health insurance industry are also in opposition to the process. (For more detailed information you are urged to obtain the Rohrers' book and Morton Walker's book, which describes in detail the status of chelation therapy in the Unitd States.)

EDTA chelation therapy is being used successfully in treating many different illnesses in which the common underlying cause of these various diseases is calcium deposited where it does not belong. The reader may be wondering if there have been known fatalities as a result of its use. The answer to that is no. The risk factor is much less than bypass surgery or other forms of conventional medical treatment.

Chelated Mineral Supplements

It is known that there are at least 117 different ways that deficiency in a single mineral can cause disease in our bodies. The body contains 96 times more minerals by weight than vitamins, so the need for minerals cannot be overstated. As has been explained, many people cannot perform the chelating process efficiently in their bodies. The need for taking mineral-nutrients, therefore, exists. But even these may be poorly absorbed. Is there an answer?

The answer is chelated mineral supplements (available through most health-food stores). These are similar to what the body makes with amino acids, and absorption problems are much less.

Those of us in the preventive health field strongly urge individuals to have a hair analysis, which is a highly accurate and painless method of scientifically evaluating the levels of nutritional minerals and toxic metals in the body. This is a valuable diagnostic tool. Delbert J. Eatough, the director of the Center for Thermochemical Studies at Brigham Young University in Provo, Utah, states:

> We've known for years that a number of illnesses, including cancer, cause changes in the levels of various minerals in the body. And for many years, doctors have been working to find

which diseases affect which minerals and to what extent. We've known that these changes can be detected in hair.[5]

Since mineral balance is such an important key to good health and total well-being, the maintenance of that balance is essential. Hair analysis is an important preventive step. If your local health-food store or local medical library cannot supply information about where you can have this done, turn to the reference section of this book for laboratories and their addresses to whom you can write for information.

Since vitamin and mineral requirements vary with the age of a person and his or her own special medical history, the reader is well-advised to exercise discretion. The charts in Appendix 1 of this book can be helpful.

FOOTNOTES

1. Dr. Richard A. Passwater, *Cancer and Its Nutritional Therapies* (New Canaan, Con.: Keats Publishing Co., 1978), p. 2.
2. Ibid., p. 3.
3. Dr. Roger J. Williams, *Nutrition Against Disease* (New York: Bantum Books, 1978), p. 41.
4. Morton Walker, D.P.M., *Total Health* (New York: Everest House, 1979), p. 96.
5. Ibid., p. 111.

12

Behold, I will bring . . .
health and cure, and I will
cure them, and will reveal
unto them the abundance
of peace and truth.
—Jeremiah 33:6

The Power of Prayer

The daughter of the college professor mentioned in chapter 9—the man in whom two brain tumors were discovered—wrote a letter in which she stated, "So many people are praying for my father. . . . It is good to know the Lord in times like this."

How true her words are! Those of us who have been through deep-water experiences can testify to that.

> When you pass through the waters I will be with you; and through the rivers, they will not overflow you. When you walk through the fire you will not be scorched, nor will the flame burn you. —(Isaiah 43:2).

Regardless of the outcome—whether God says, "yes," "No," "Wait," or "I have some other plan"—there is a certain strength and peace that comes in quite no way other than as we pray and leave the outcome to God. When we talk it over with the Lord, asking for a return to health, but asking for His perfect will to be accomplished in our lives, then a quiet confidence seeps into our entire being, leaving us with that calm assurance that God does know the end from the beginning, and that He indeed does all things well.

What we do forget, however, in our well days is that God has issued warnings throughout the Bible telling us to pay attention to Him, and when we do, He will not forget to help us (cf. Isaiah 44:21 TLB).

What's the Good of Prayer?

Someone may question, "What's the good of prayer? If God has already made up His mind about me, why pray?" God has given us a free will; He will not force Himself or His will upon us. But the Bible does tell us that God moves in response to our praying. The inner man needs nourishment, just as the physical man requires this for sustenance. We can either starve that inner man or nourish it, and prayer is one of the ways by which we nourish the inner spirit. Too many of us regard praying as a means of getting something for self; the biblical emphasis on prayer is that we may draw closer to God and, in so doing, come to know Him better. To meditate and pray is to allow a power greater than self to move into one's being and to alter one's attitude and disposition.

As one woman was faced with the knowledge that she had cancer, she said, "Whether I die, I win either way." Such assurance is the result of knowing God intimately and trusting in His Son and the biblical promise that there is life in the hereafter. Death becomes the stepping-stone to something more and something better that will last forever.

The Psalmist knew what it was to come under affliction. In one place he groaned, "My eye has wasted away because of affliction" (Psalm 88:9a NASB). Tears are very therapeutic. The Bible tells us that God keeps a record of them. They are precious in His sight. Psalm 102 records a longer prayer of a man who was afflicted and overwhelmed. He begins as an unpardoned man and tells what effect this kind of living has had on his health; the very next psalm tells of release:

> Who pardons all your iniquities, who heals all your diseases.
> —Psalm 103:3 NASB

The Bible contains many accounts of miraculous healings.

God does sometimes heal both instantaneously and miraculously, and also healing comes with time as he uses the skills of dedicated doctors and medical science. Neither should be discounted. God will provide healing in answer to prayer and as the afflicted individual cooperates with Him and does the right things to bring about a return to health. Originally God provided a world in perfect balance, as we have seen. The only requirement He made for its preservation in that state was simple obedience. A free exercise of personal responsibility would have maintained that state. Now we are confronted with ecological imbalance and many other un-wholistic side effects.

But God did not leave man in his dilemma. He continued to provide do's and don't's which included personal as well as community responsibilities for maintenance of health (cf. Leviticus 11; Deuteronomy 14; Leviticus 13-15; Deuteronomy 23). God told the people what to do and what not to do to minimize disease. Still later, Jesus, whose caring qualities run throughout the Gospel narratives, appeared on the scene, and there was healing in His touch. We never read of Jesus in ill health. The mandate He gave to His disciples (and that includes all who would be His followers) was to tell others about the love of God *and* to heal the sick. One reading of the book of Acts is convincing proof that those first disciples really took Jesus at His word, and that physical and spiritual healing resulted.

The early church did not forget Christ's words; for centuries a hallmark characteristic of these Christians was their love and concern for others. Saint Augustine, in his prayers and writings, referred to his Maker as "Thou, my inmost Physician." Augustine's *Confessions* reveal that he knew what it was to be afflicted:

> Woe is me! Lord, have pity on me.
> My evil sorrows strive with my good joys;
> and on which side is the victory, I know not.
> Woe is me! Lord, have pity on me.
> Woe is me! lo! I hide not my wounds;

Thou art the Physician, I the sick;
Thou merciful, I miserable.
Is not the life of man upon earth all trial?
Who wishes for troubles and difficulties?
Thou commandest them to be endured, not to be loved.
No man loves what he endures, though he love to endure.
For though he rejoices that he endures, he had rather there
were nothing for him to endure. . . .
And all my hope is nowhere but in Thy exceeding great
mercy.[1]

But Augustine's experience, as well as the experiences of countless numbers of saints past and present, reveals a man in communication with God.

All Things Are Possible Through Prayer

Dr. Charles L. Allen, much-respected theologian and author, has written a book of timeless quality entitled *All Things Are Possible Through Prayer*. But he would be the first to tell you that the title was not original with him. It is a book which every searching soul should read. Throughout the Bible we are reminded of the truth that all things are possible through prayer. At one point, in a discussion with His disciples, Jesus made the statement, ". . . with God all things are possible" (Matthew 19:26).

Still later, He once again emphasized this vital truth: "All things are possible to him who believes" (Mark 9:23 NASB). This is a thread woven throughout the New Testament.

Dr. Allen relates many interesting stories; one in particular outlines the attitude we can take in regard to sickness and tragedy. He tells of Sir Harry Lauder, a great comedian in his day. When news came that his son had been killed, Sir Lauder, after thinking through the tragedy, concluded: "In a time like this there are three courses open to a man: 1) he may give way to despair, sour upon the world, and become a grouch; 2) he may endeavor to drown his sorrows in drink or by a life of waywardness and wickedness; 3) he may turn to God." The grieving father took the third course and allowed the sorrow to refine his faith, thereby finding life's greatest meaning. Dr. Allen remarked, "He kept the pain but gained the power to endure the pain, and that in itself is a high form of healing."[2]

Prayer Is No Cure-All

Leslie D. Weatherhead *(Prescription for Anxiety)* reminds us that prayer is no cure-all. "If it were, medical, psychological, and other forms of research would become unnecessary. Further, the aim of praying is unity with God and not merely regaining of one's health. Prayer is degraded if, when medicine, surgery and psychology fail, we do what a man once described to me as 'trying a spot of prayer.' "

The help of professionals in the field of research, medicine, and psychology is not to be minimized. Serious anxiety and tormenting fear may indeed require the help of a psychiatrist. But the help to be found in taking one's eyes off one's own problems and turning them to God is to be emphasized. Consider for example these brief sentences:

> The Lord is my shepherd. . . . Thou art with me.
>
> The Lord is my light and my salvation; whom shall I fear? The Lord is the strength of my life; of whom shall I be afraid?
>
> Wait on the Lord: be of good courage, and He shall strengthen thine heart. . . .
>
> The eyes of the Lord are upon the righteous, and His ears are open unto their cry.
>
> And now, Lord, what wait I for? My hope is in Thee. . . . Hear my prayer, O Lord, and give ear unto my cry; hold not Thy peace at my tears. . . . O spare me, that I may recover strength. . . .
>
> The Lord will strengthen . . . upon the bed of languishing. . .
>
> God is our refuge and strength, a very present help in trouble. Therefore will not we fear.
>
> For this God is our God for ever and ever: He will be our guide even unto death.
>
> Behold, God is my helper. . . .

Cast thy burden upon the Lord, and He shall sustain thee. . . .

Thy mercy is great unto the heavens. . . .

Trust in Him at all times; ye people, pour out your heart before Him: God is a refuge for us.

Prayer Prepares Us

What confidence such words inspire! And these are just a few random verses selected from the book of Psalms. How much we deprive ourselves of help and hope by a neglect of the Bible and prayer!

While prayer is not a cure-all, it is the means by which we commune with God. Prayer prepares us for whatever faces us. Too many people, however, come to God seeking a handout, as if He were to be regarded only as some kind of benevolent "big Daddy." No wonder their prayers go unanswered!

Jesus gave us the example of how to approach the Father in prayer. The Gospels abound with these examples of the Son in prayer to the Father. After Jesus spoke to the Father, voicing His requests, He didn't forget to thank Him. "Father, I thank Thee that Thou has heard Me" (John 11:41).

The Importance of Having a Thankful Heart

There is a very pointed lesson in the Bible about the importance of having a thankful heart. Interestingly enough, it relates to healing of the sick. Ten lepers met Jesus in a small village. They cried out to Him for mercy. Jesus gave them a very simple instruction: they were to go and show themselves to the priests. "And as they went they were cured and made clean" (Luke 17:14 AMP).

You would have thought that they would come rushing back to Jesus to show Him what had happened, and to thank Him. Not so. Only one of them recognized what had happened and began thanking and praising God with a loud voice (v. 15). The next scene shows him falling prostrate at the feet of Jesus, "thanking Him (over and over)" (AMP).

Notice Jesus' words "Were not ten cleansed? Where are

the nine?'' (v. 17 AMP). I wonder if there was a note of sadness in Jesus' voice "Was there no one found to return and to recognize and give thanks and praise to God except this alien?" (v. 18 AMP). (The reference to "alien" was that the man was a Samaritan, despised in that particular region of Galilee.)

Very kindly Jesus said to the man, "Get up and go on your way. Your faith [that is, your trust and confidence that spring from your belief in God] has restored you to health" (v. 19 AMP).

I think this is tremendously significant. First we see Jesus asking the lepers to do something which they did. This is *obedience*. Matthew Henry observes that if we do what we can , God will not be lacking to do for us what we cannot do. In regards to our physical well-being, that is worth remembering. Second, we see one man, and one only, returning immediately to give thanks. No doubt he had often lifted up his voice in prayer asking God to heal him; now he has experienced it. Once again he lifts up his voice in a loud "Glory to God!" and thanks and praises God for this miracle of healing. Note also that the man lost no time in thanking God for his mercy. Sometimes a time lag dulls our sense of the greatness of what has happened. We must remember to be quick to give God the glory due Him.

But then notice, third, the abundance of healing available from Christ. Ten lepers were healed. There is a sufficiency in Jesus that never runs out. But how poor these nine were in returning gratitude! How common that is, however. Ingratitude is a very common sin. We are daily recipients of God's many mercies, but how few there are who acknowledge this. In compassion God heard the cries of these ten distressed men, and in mercy He answered their pleas for healing. We have no record that Jesus took their healing away from them because of their ingratitude, but we do see that this one man was distinguished from the rest in a special way.

We need to remember to thank God for our health. The

Father is pleased with our thanksgiving. We also need to ask Him to keep us in good health, and to show us ways by which we can cooperate with Him in the maintenance of a state of wellness.

Live One Day at a Time

We believe that God will respond to the person who earnestly seeks to respond to the clear mandates of the Word and will live according to its plain teachings. In our human understanding of disease, we have often been guilty of leaving God out of the picture. We need to regain a healthy respect for biblical laws governing health; a return to moderation in our diets is long overdue. Furthermore, as a nation we violate the weekly day of rest commanded by God in the Bible. We are to rest from physical and mental work. We are to worship God, and in so doing we are to receive guidance, encouragement, and help, and to share in fellowship with other believers. God has promised to bless those who remember to observe His commandments. This is immensely important for physical, mental, and spiritual health.

Turning once again to the New Testament, we see Jesus, in that great Sermon on the Mount, setting forth precepts that are timeless. Can the individual confronted with cancer, coronary, or some other disease find help there? Jesus' counsel to His listeners was then and is still today meant to be heeded. (Read Matthew 5, 6, and 7).

"Don't worry about things," is what Jesus said. Your anxiety and fears will not extend your life; in fact, anxious worry is the worst thing you can do to yourself. Jesus called attention to the birds, and to the field lilies—simple things—and then He said, "You are far more valuable to the Father than birds." That's a profound thought, for who among us hasn't watched a bird in flight, or in search of food, and marveled at these winged creatures? Jesus said, "Your heavenly Father feeds them." Then Jesus added: "Will all your worries add a single moment to your life? . . . If God cares so wonderfully for flowers that are here today and gone tomorrow, won't he more surely care for you? . . . So don't be anxious about tomorrow. God will take care of your tomorrow too. Live one day at a time'' (Matthew 6:27,30,34, TLB).

John Wesley, zealous for the faith, in one of his many writings recorded these few lines. They are memorable; and as we think of ways in which we can cooperate with God in preventing coronary, cancer, and other diseases, we will do well to reflect on these and other thoughts that can make us receptive to health.

> My remnant of days
> I spend to His praise
> Who died the whole world to redeem:
> Be they many or few,
> My days are His due,
> And they all are devoted to Him.

He who made your body, can remake you even now if you are unwell. He still hears and answers prayers. And there is great power in prayer. But some diseases will have to wait the final cure in heaven. One day there will be a great resurrection and we shall all have new bodies—those who have trusted in the Savior. God will cure disease; He will bring health and cure, He will reveal the abundance of peace and truth (Jeremiah 33:6)—it may be in the here and now; or it may be in the hereafter. Remember, disease is not His perfect will. God's answer is *prevent it.*

FOOTNOTES

1. Translated by E.B. Pusey, *The Confessions of St. Augustine* (out-of-print translation), p. 248.
2. Dr. Charles L. Allen, *All Things Are Possible Through Prayer* (Old Tappan, N.J.: Fleming H. Revell Co., 1958), p. 118.

Appendices

APPENDIX 1

VITAMINS AND MINERALS

TABLE OF NUTRIENT FUNCTIONS

MINERALS
TABLE OF NUTRIENT FUNCTION

NUTRIENT	BENEFITS—ACCEPTED	BENEFITS—PLAUSIBLE	COFACTORS
Calcium	Most abundant mineral in the body. Sustains strong bones and teeth; aids blood clotting; helps maintain blood pH; cardiovascular health, normal pulse and cardiac contraction, normal nerve function, muscle growth and contraction; helps activate enzymes; aids iron utilization and cell-membrane stability; helps regulate nutrient passage through cell walls; acts as natural tranquilizer and painkiller.	Treatment of insomnia, osteoporosis, cardiovascular disorders, foot or leg cramps, "growing pains"; prevention or treatment of sunburn; protection against sun-caused cancers; used with vitamin A as neutralizing agent against poison of black widow, spider, or bee stings; treatment of arthritis and rheumatism; used with magnesium and vitamin D for problems of menopause, rickets, osteomalacia, menstrual cramps, premenstrual tension, nephritis, tooth and gum disorders; protection against radioactive strontium 90, aging (bone pain, backaches, insomnia, brittle teeth with cavities, finger tremors).	Vitamin A Vitamin C Vitamin D Vitamin F Iron Magnesium (2 parts calcium to 1 part magnesium) Manganese Phosphorus (2.5 parts calcium to 1 part phosphorus) Hydrochloric acid Protein

NUTRIENT	BENEFITS—ACCEPTED	BENEFITS—PLAUSIBLE	COFACTORS
Chlorine	Occurs in the body mainly in compound form with sodium or potassium. Regulates blood pH; maintains osmotic pressure of cell membranes; stimulates hydrochloric acid production; maintains healthy joints and tendons; stimulates liver function; helps distribute hormones.	Treatment of diarrhea, vomiting.	No information available.
Chromium	Trace element. Stimulates enzymes in metabolism of energy and synthesis of fatty acids, cholesterol, and protein; helps transport protein in blood; aids insulin; helps to regulate blood sugar.	May be involved in synthesis of protein through its binding action with RNA molecules; Prevents or lowers high blood pressure; reduces cholesterol and hardening of the arteries; helps fight mental changes accompanying senility; therapeutic value to diabetics and other abnormal glucose-tolerance conditions.	None known.
Cobalt	Trace element. Integral part of vitamin B-12. Maintains red blood cells; activates a number of enzymes in the body.	Treatment of pernicious anemia.	Copper Iron Zinc
Copper	Trace mineral. Part of many enzymes; facilitates hemoglobin formation and iron absorption; helps form elastin; aids conversion of tyrosine into pigment for hair and skin; aids in protein metabolism, healing processes, phospholipids synthesis, bone formation and maintenance, and RNA production.	Aids vitamin E. Treatment of anemia, edema, kwashiorkor.	Cobalt Iron Zinc

Fluorine	Occurs as fluorides. Essential trace mineral; sodium fluoride is added to drinking water; reduces tooth decay.	Increases deposition of calcium, thereby strengthening bones.	None known.
Iodine	Trace mineral. Converted to iodide in the body. Prevents goiter; regulates metabolic rate; promotes growth and thyroxine production; aids development and function of thyroid, mentality, speech, condition of hair, nails, skin and teeth; aids conversion of carotene into vitamin A, synthesis of protein by ribosomes, absorption of carbohydrates from intestines, synthesis of cholesterol, and treatment of cretinism.	Prevents hardening of the arteries; reduces danger of radioactive iodine collecting in thyroid.	No information available.
Iron	All iron exists in the body combined with protein. Iron is a mineral concentrate present in every living cell. Aids hemoglobin and myoglobin formation; promotes growth; aids in stress and disease tolerance; present in enzymes that promote protein metabolism; with other nutrients, improves cell respiratory action; prevents anemia during menstruation; treats anemia.	Treatment of leukemia, colitis.	Vitamin B12 Folic acid Vitamin C Calcium Cobalt Copper Phosphorus Hydrochloric acid
Magnesium	Present in all living tissues. Activates more enzymes in the body than any other mineral. With calcium and phosphorus, forms strong bones and teeth; aids muscle contraction;	Added to megavitamin therapy in treating emotional illness; prevention and treatment of heart disease; regulation of body temperature; prevents calcium and phosphor-	Vitamin B6 Vitamin C Vitamin D Protein

NUTRIENT	BENEFITS—ACCEPTED	BENEFITS—PLAUSIBLE	COFACTORS
	serves as catalyst in utilization of carbohydrates, fats, protein, calcium, phosphorus, sodium, and potassium; regulates body's acid-alkali balance; helps utilize B-complex and vitamins C and E; antacid; aids in permeability of cell membranes; transmission of nerve impulses; liver in storing sugar as glycogen and releasing it for energy; with hormone cortisone, regulates blood phosphate; vital to body's immune system.	us stones in urinary tract; helps reduce blood cholesterol; control of convulsions in in epileptics. Treatment of prostrate troubles, polio, depression, neuromuscular disorders, nervousness, tantrums, sensitivity to noise, hand tremor, control of delirium tremens in alcoholics, hyperthyroidism, diarrhea, vomiting, kwashiorkor, kidney disease, kidney stones, gallstones.	Calcium (1 part magnesium to 2 parts calcium) Phosphorus (usually too much is supplied in the diet for the proper calcium-phosphorus-magnesium ratio)
Manganese	Trace mineral, vital for normal skeletal development, protein-carbohydrate-fat production, choline utilization and activities, biotin, thiamine, and vitamin C utilization, synthesis of fatty acids and cholesterol, hemoglobin formation, production of milk in lactation, formation of urea; nourishes nerves and brain.	Functioning of vitamin E; with B-complex, relieves devastating weakness by stimulating transmission of impulses between nerve and muscles; treatment of diabetes, since manganese may be involved in manufacturing insulin. Treatment of myasthenia gravis and multiple sclerosis.	Vitamin B-complex Vitamin B1 Vitamin E Calcium Phosphorus
Molybdenum	Trace mineral. As an essential part of two enzymes, acts in oxidation of fats and aldehydes and aids in mobilization of iron from liver reserves.	Prevention of anemia (exerts a stimulatory effect on hemoglobin regeneration when used concurrently with iron therapy).	No information available.
Phosphorus	Second most abundant mineral in the body. Found in every cell of the body. Performs more functions than any other mineral in the body. Aids in carbohydrate, fat, and protein utilization; with calcium, builds bones &	Speeds up bone mending and reduces calcium loss from fractures; prevents or cures rickets; prevents stunted growth. helps in cancer prevention; prevents dental cavities. Treatment of osteomalacia, osteoporosis,	Vitamin A Vitamin D Vitamin F Calcium (1 part phosphorus to 2.5 parts calcium)

	teeth; stimulates muscle contractions, including heart; aids in digestion of niacin and riboflavin; part of nucleoproteins; aids in normal kidney functioning, nerve impulse transfer; in phospholipids (such as lecithin) helps break up and transport fats and fatty acids; helps maintain blood pH; assists in the passage of substances through the cell walls; promotes the secretion of glandular hormones; promotes healthy nerves and efficient mental activity.	arthritis related to stress, and disorders of the teeth and gums.	Iron Manganese Protein
Potassium	Essential to growth, nerve-impulse transmission, muscle contraction, proper pH alkalinity of body fluids; maintains healthy skin; aids in conversion of glucose to glycogen, cell metabolism, enzyme reactions, synthesis of muscle protein from amino acids; stimulates kidneys to eliminate body wastes; with phosphorus, sends oxygen to the brain; with calcium, influences the contractability of smooth, skeletal, and cardiac muscles; with sodium, regulates distribution of cellular fluid, and nourishes the muscular system.	Treatment of high blood pressure due to excessive salt intake; diabetes (can reduce blood-pressure and blood-sugar levels); headaches; diarrhea; (as potassium chloride) Colic in infant; (as postassium chloride) allergies. Used to slow heartbeat in severe injury, such as burns.	B6 Sodium
Selenium	Preserves tissue elasticity; detoxifies mercury; with protein, treats kwashiorkor; with vitamin E; aids in metabolic action promotion of normal body growth and fertility.	Can replace vitamin E if necessary; with vitamin E; stimulates the body's immune response; with vitamins E and C, acts as an antioxidant, protects against carcinogen-induced cancers, (especially in digestive tract) and sun-induced skin cancer; with	Vitamin E

NUTRIENT	BENEFITS—ACCEPTED	BENEFITS—PLAUSIBLE	COFACTORS
Sodium	Maintains nervous, muscular, blood, and lymph systems; maintains cellular fluid; keeps other blood minerals soluble so they will not build up as deposits in the bloodstream; aids in carbon dioxide elimination and hydrochloric acid production; with chlorine, improves blood and lymph health; with potassium, equalizes blood pH; with potassium, aids muscle contraction and expansion and nerve stimulation.	magnesium and zinc, prevents heart disease. Resistance to heat cramps & stroke. Treatment of toxemia, edema, proteinuria, and blurred vision.	Vitamin D Chlorine Potassium
Vanadium	Reduces cholesterol; aids in fat metabolism, natural circulatory-regulating system, and amino acid conversion.	Preventing tooth decay.	No information available.
Zinc	Aids in carbohydrate digestion and phosphorus metabolism; component of insulin and male reproductive fluid; aids in wound and burn healing; normalizes absorption and actions of vitamins, especially B-complex; constituent of at least 25 enzymes involved in digestion, metabolism, and tissue respiration; aids in nucleic acid synthesis, bone growth, and growth and development of reproductive organs; normal function of prostate gland; mobilizes vitamin A from the liver.	Stimulates appetite; inhibits cancer; aids in DNA synthesis; eliminates cholesterol artery deposits; aids in rapid healing and in fertility; included in megavitamin treatment of emotional illness; with selenium and magnesium, sustains healthy hearts; beneficial to the diabetic because of its regulatory affect in insulin in the blood (a diabetic pancreas contains only about ½ as much zinc as does a healthy one). Treatment of Hodgkin's disease, leukemia, alcoholism, cirrhosis of the liver, anemia short stature due to glandular defects, skin sores, liver and	Vitamin A Copper Phosphorus

spleen problems, arteriosclerosis, sickle-cell anemia, gastric ulcers, venous and ischemic leg ulcers, acrodermatitis, enteropathica (AE), and rheumatoid arthritis.

Essential trace minerals, role in human nutrition unknown:

Boron
Lithium
Silicon
Strontium
Tin
Tritium

Minerals that are not essential, found in the body, function unknown:

Nickel

Minerals dangerous, but often found in the human body:

Aluminum
Beryllium
Cadmium
Lead
Mercury

VITAMINS

TABLE OF NUTRIENT FUNCTIONS

NUTRIENT	BENEFITS—ACCEPTED	BENEFITS—PLAUSIBLE	COFACTORS
Vitamin A	Fat-soluble. "Tissue growth and repair; healthy eyes; healthy epithelial tissue; fights bacteria; bone and teeth formation; gastric juice secretion; rich blood; protects mucous membranes from infection and air pollutants; forms visual purple; reproduction.	Prevents viruses, prevents cancerous cells; shortens communicable disease duration; reduces high cholestrol atheroma. Treatment of asthma, chronic rhinitis, dermatitis, tuberculosis, emphysema, gastritis, hyperthyroidism, nephritis, tinnitus, migraine, liver cirrhosis, blurred vision, night blindness, cataracts, crossed eyes, nearsightedness, glaucoma, conjunctivitis, xerophthalmia. Externally: acne, impetigo, boils, carbuncles, open ulcers, wounds. By injection: removal of plantar's warts.	Vitamin B complex Choline Vitamin C Vitamin D Vitamin E Vitamin F Calcium Phosphorus Zinc
Vitamin B1 (thiamine)	Water-soluble. Healthy nervous system; growth; improves muscle tone of internal organs; stabilizes appetite; decreases edema; reduces enlarged hearts; eliminates motion sickness; alleviates fatigue; carbohydrate metabolism. Treatment of alcoholism, herpes zoster.	Overcomes enzyme deficiencies; improves mental acuity; multiple sclerosis treatment.	B-complex Folic acid Vitamin B2 Niacin Vitamin C Vitamin E Manganese Sulfur
Vitamin B2 (riboflavin)	Water-soluble. Nutrient metabolism; healthy eyes, skin, nails, and hair; aids enzyme systems; iron absorption; cell respiration; growth and development.	Improves mental acuity; inhibits cancer; corrects enzyme deficiencies; lessens anxiety; aids antibody and red-blood-cell formation; promotes healthy thyroid; eye-problem prevention. Treatment of eye problems and eczema.	Vitamin B-complex Vitamin B6 Niacin Vitamin C

Vitamin B3 (niacin)	Forms: nicotinic acid, nicotinamide; niacinamide. Niacin equivalent: 60 mg. tryptophan (an essential amino acid) can form 1 gram niacin in the body.	Healthy skin, tongue, and nervous and digestive systems; sex hormone synthesis; cell respiration; enzyme systems component; metabolic aid; hydrochloric acid production; reduces high blood pressure; increases circulation. Treatment of acne, migraine, schizophrenia, pellagra, delirium, diarrhea.	B-complex Vitamin B1 Vitamin B2 Vitamin C
Vitamin B5	(Calcium panthothenate, pantothenic acid). Water-soluble. Fights stress, fights fatigue; vitamin utilization; fat formation; carbohydrate, fat, and protein metabolism; adrenal function; reduces antibiotic toxicity.	Prevents nerve degeneration; protects against radiation; retards aging; improves mental acuity; corrects enzyme deficiencies; arthritis treatment.	Vitamin B-complex Vitamin B6 Vitamin B12 Biotin Folic acid Vitamin C Sulfur
Vitamin B6	(Pyridoxine and pyridoxal, from vegetable sources; pyridoxamine from animal sources). Water-soluble. Niacin production; protein, carbohydrate and fat metabolism; lecithin production; antibody and red-blood-cell formation; B12 partner; sodium and phosphorus balance.	Treatment of mental disorders, arthritis, edema, atherosclerosis, nausea of pregnancy, ulcers, anemia, rheumatism, diabetes, menstrual and menopausal disorders, convulsions, epilepsy, nervous-system disease, cancer, weak or stiff muscles, eczema, hair loss, motion sickness, hand tremors, palsy, sexual disorders, diarrhea, hemorrhoids, tooth decay, high cholesterol, acne, pancreatitis, kidney stones, Parkinson's disease.	Vitamin B-complex Vitamin B1 Vitamin B2 Pantothenic acid Vitamin C Magnesium Potassium Linoleic acid Sodium
Vitamin B12	(Cyanocobalamin). Water-soluble. Aids metabolism; benefits anemias; aids growth and functioning of cells, especially in bone marrow, nervous system, and gastrointestinal tract. Relief of fatigue, irritability, mem-	Heart-disease prevention; antiviral action; menstrual regulation; growth in children. Treatment of emotional disorders, bloodvessel disease in elderly, nervous-system tumors (cancer), displaced spinal disc,	Vitamin B complex Vitamin B6 Choline Folic acid Inositol

NUTRIENT	BENEFITS—ACCEPTED	BENEFITS—PLAUSIBLE	COFACTORS
	ory impairment, inability to concentrate, depression, insomnia, lack of balance. Treatment of sprue, osteoarthritis, osteoporsis, "tobacco amblyopia."	skin disease, asthma, shingles, hepatitis, bursitis.	Vitamin C Potassium Sodium
Biotin	Water-soluble. Fat, carbohydrate, and protein metabolism; aids B-vitamin and protein utilization; normal growth.	Treatment of dermatitis and baldness.	Vitamin B-complex Vitamin B12 Folic acid Pantothenic acid Vitamin C Sulfur
Choline	Water-soluble. Nerve transmission; liver, kidney, and arterial health; liver and gallbladder functioning; aids metabolism and fat transportation; thyroid hormone manufacture.	Reduces high blood pressure; disolves fat and cholesterol. Treatment of heart palpitation, dizziness, headaches, ear ringing, constipation, insomnia, visual disturbances, blood flow to eyes, glaucoma, liver damage; hepatitis, kidney damage, kidney hemorrhaging, nephritis, psychiatric diseases, depression.	Vitamin A B-complex Vitamin B12 Folic acid Inositol Linoleic acid
Inositol	Water-soluble. Fat metabolism; reduces cholesterol; prevents artery disease; prevents hair loss.	Mild inhibitory effect on cancer; appetite stimulant. Treatment of eczema, dermatitis, constipation, fatty infiltration of liver, liver cirrhosis.	Vitamin B-complex Choline Linoleic acid
Folic Acid (Folacin)	Water-soluble. Choline synthesis; amino-acid metabolism and B12 function; anemia prevention; growth and reproduction; red-blood-cell production; blood-clotting aid;	Improves circulation; repairs arteries; aids atherosclerotic lesions and gout. Treatment of diarrhea, sprue, dropsy, stomach ulcers, menstrual problems, leg ulcers,	Vitamin B-complex Vitamin B12 Biotin Pantothenic acid

	appetite aid; stimulates hydrochloric acid production.	tongue inflammation.	Vitamin C
PABA	(Para-aminobenzoic acid). Water-soluble. Occurs naturally in combination with folic acid; red blood cell formation; utilization of proteins; stimulates intestinal bacteria to produce folic acid; applied to the skin, acts as sunscreen and soothes pain of burns.	Prevents graying hair; antiarthritic. Treatment of vitiligo, some parasitic diseases, Rocky Mountain spotted fever.	Vitamin B-complex Vitamin C Folic acid
Bioflavonoids (vitamin P)	Water-soluble. The compounds of bioflavonoids are citrin, hesperidin, rutin, flavones, and flavonals. Absorption of Vitamin C; capillary strength; capillary permeability; assists C in collagen regulation.	Prevents infection, colds, and flu; prevents hemorrhages and ruptures in capillaries and connective tissues; minimizes bruising; strengthens vessel walls; protects against X-rays; prevents miscarriages. Treatment of capillary injury, hemorrhoids, tendency to hemorrhaging, duodenal ulcers, labyrinthitis, asthma, bleeding gums, eczema, rheumatism, rheumatic fever, blood-vessel disorders of eye, muscular dystrophy.	Vitamin C
Vitamin C	(Ascorbic acid). Water-soluble. Metabolism of amino acids, absorption of iron, activity of folic acid; combats stress, repairs cells; prevents scurvy; healthy bones, teeth, and capillary walls; manufacture of collagen; infection resistance; healing; activates the adrenal glands; eases pain of spinal disc injuries; nonsurgical care in spinal disc lesions, knee cartilage damage, sacroiliac damage.	Combats common cold; sharpens mental abilities; slows aging through collagen production; combats emotional disorders; lowers cholesterol and reduces arthritic pain; prevents and/or counteracts poisoning from lead, arsenic, carbon monoxide, benzene, bromides, and severe toxins such as poison ivy or poison oak; burn healing applied to skin and to bacterial and viral infections; resists cancer growth. Treatment	All vitamins and minerals Bioflavonoids Calcium Magnesium

NUTRIENT	BENEFITS—ACCEPTED	BENEFITS—PLAUSIBLE	COFACTORS
		of whooping cough, prickly heat, inflammation of the urethra, hypoglycemia, cataracts, back problems, shock, gastric hemorrhage, arthritis, pernicious anemia, iron-deficiency anemia, duodenal ulcer.	
Vitamin D	Fat-soluble. Two forms most important in nutrition: D2—man-made, by irradiating ergosterol; D3—natural, from fish-liver oils. Prevents or cures rickets; repairs osteomalacia. Necessary for normal growth strong bones and teeth, absorption and utilization of calcium and phosphorus, which with vitamin D maintains a stable nervous system and normal heart action.	Epilepsy control; tooth decay and pyorrhea; combined with vitamins A & C, reduces colds; eliminates stomach ulcers by reducing acidity of gastric juices; reduction in myopia; combined with calcium, relief from chronic conjunctivitis; treatment of keratoconus.	Vitamin A (10 parts A to 1 part D) Vitamin C Vitamin F Choline Calcium Phosphorus
Vitamin K	K1 and K2 are made within the body; K3 is synthetic. Fat-soluble. Normal blood clotting; reduces operative blood loss; normal liver functioning; normal menstruation.	Painkiller; cancer prevention; lowers high blood pressure; used with anticoagulant drugs for heart conditions.	No information available at this time.
Vitamin E	Fat-soluble. Group of 7 compounds called tocopherols, of which alpha tocopherol is the most potent form and has the greatest nutritional and biological value. Prevents oxidaton of vitamins A, C, and polyunsaturated fatty acids; interrelated with selenium function; cell production and repair; protects against poisonous chemicals; aids oxygen absorption; aids circulation; protects pituitary and adrenal hormones; nor-	Counteracts oxidant damage to lung membranes; retards aging; cancer-inhibiting; prevents or dissolves blood clots; improves circulation; increases sperm quality; fights kidney disease; aids damaged liver; with vitamin A, lowers cholesterol; prevents miscarriages. Treatment of bursitis, gout, arthritis, nearsightedness, crossed eyes, muscular dystrophy, vascular degeneration of gangrene in diabetics, migraine head-	Vitamin A B-complex Vitamin B1 Inositol Vitamin C Vitamin F Manganese Selenium (effectiveness decreased by Iron and choline)

malizes scar-tissue formation. Treatment of edema, elevated blood pressure, cyanosis, angina pectoris, intermittent claudication, rheumatic heart disease in its early stages of cardiac complications, atherosclerosis (if **vitamin E is begun before irreparable** damage has occurred), irregular menses, menopausal symptoms, varicose veins, thrombosis; helps regulate the metabolism of fats and proteins.

aches; promotes collateral circulation in varicose veins; external use in treatment of burns, skin ulcers, and abrasions; combats acute kidney inflammation, acute rheumatic fever, coronary and cerebral thrombosis, thrombophlebitis, emotional or physical strains that may create breathing problems, purpura, retinitis, premature detachment of the placenta; increases platelets in bloodstream (essential to blood clotting).

APPENDIX 2

International Academy of Preventive Medicine
10409 Town and Country Way, Suite 200
Houston, Texas 77024

International College of Applied Nutrition
P.O. Box 368
La Habra, California 90631

National Health Federation
212 West Foothill Boulevard
Monrovia, California 91016

American Orthomolecular Psychiatry
1691 Northen Boulevard
Manhasset, New York 11030

Society for Clinical Ecology
4045 Wadwarth Boulevard
Wheat Ridge, Colorado 80033

American Academy of Medical Preventics
2811 "L" Street
Sacramento, California 95816

American Institute of Homeopathy
6231 Leesburg Pike, Suite 56
Falls Church, Virginia 72044

Committee for Freedom of Choice in Cancer Therapy
146 Main Street #408
Los Altos, California 94022

Cancer Control Society
2043 North Berendo
Los Angeles, California 91016

International Association of Cancer Victims and Friends
Box 707
Solana Beach, California 92075

AID Laboratory (early cancer-detection testing)
Suite 606-E & F, Sherman Plaza
605 South Sherman Street
Richardson, Texas 75081

International Preventive Medicine Foundation
M-S325, P.O. Box 42999
Houston, Texas 77042

APPENDIX 3

This is a summary table for the therapeutic augmentation of concentrated nutrients that can assure most people of an ample supply of what the cells need for a cell-assurance program.

These are general recommendations for good nutrition-wise food fortifiers, and in no way are they to be considered as personal prescribing for anyone. This is best left up to your doctor after a good checkup.

Vitamin A, oil capsules	20,000-30,000 units per day
Vitamin A, micro-emulsion	50,000 units per day
Vitamin C	2000-6000 mg. per day
Vitamin D	400-1000 units per day
Gluco-Min	1 3x per day
Vitamin E capsules	200-800 units per day
Selenium tablets	50-150 mg. per day
B-complex tablets or capsules	1 3x per day
Digestive tablets	1 2-3x per day
B17	50-100 mg. per day
B15	50-100 mg. per day
DISMU-TAB	1 3x per day
INZYME	1 3x per day
RE-ZYME	1 3x per day
Liver desiccated tabs	2 3x per day
Yeast, brewers	2 3x per day

Positify yourself by maintaining a good relationship with your Creator to maintain the confidence and assurance in your life when God prevails.